My Angel Daniel

Vassula with Her Angel Daniel

Vassula with Her Angel Daniel

This is a representation of Vassula being protected by her Guardian Angel, Daniel, who helped her draw this and four other sketches in the book.

My Angel Daniel

ANGEL, Notebooks 1–4
Vassula Ryden

Early Dawn
of
"True Life in God"

Published by

Trinitas™

Independence, Missouri, USA 64051

Declaration

The decree of the Congregation for the Propagation of the Faith, A.A.S. 58, 1186 (approved by Pope Paul VI on October 14, 1966) states that the Nihil Obstat and Imprimatur are no longer required on publications that deal with private revelations, provided they contain nothing contrary to faith and morals.

The publisher wishes to manifest unconditional submission to the final and official judgment of the Magisterium of the Church.

My Angel Daniel
Vassula Ryden
ANGEL, Notebooks 1–4

Published by

Trinitas™

P.O. Box 475
Independence, Missouri, USA 64051
Phone (816) 254-4489

Cover photo: Icon of Saint Gabriel from Saint Michael's Monastery on the Island of Simi in Greece

ISBN: 1-883225-17-5

For further information direct all inquiries to Trinitas.

Printed in United States of America.

First Printing—1995

Table of Contents

Welcome

To the praise of Jesus and Mary

Jesus asked me to tell you to always take my name, Vassula, out of the messages and replace it with your own name.

I really must express here my gratitude to my family, my spiritual director, and all my faithful friends who have made the preparation of this book possible.

I want to mention Father René Laurentin, Sr. Lucy Rooney, Father Bob Faricy, Father Michael O'Carroll, Tony Hickey, Pat Callahan, Tom Austin, and everyone who promotes and helps distribute these messages. I bless the Lord and thank Him for the ears that heard His Cry of Love from His Cross and now, touched, become His mouthpieces broadcasting this Cry of Love.

Other Titles Available
"True Life in God"

Preface

We invite you to approach this book as if Vassula Ryden were a stenographer, taking down for you a personal message of great importance given with great love. Many are already aware of and have even experienced the reality of their angels in some palpable fashion, if not in the extraordinary way that Vassula experienced hers. The Lord has indicated that He is speaking to each of us individually and tells us to take away Vassula's name in these messages and replace it with our own. Not only Vassula, but each of us has a guardian angel who is certainly as eager as hers to have us recognize that "God is near you and loves you." Vassula asked about her angel's presence on May 30, 1986 and this exchange followed: Angel Book 1:17-18

Where are you usually?

I am where you are.

Could you see me as clearly as I see things?

Yes.

Where are you when I run down the stairs?

I am with you.

Where are you now?

I am near you.

Where will you be when I die?

You will meet me; I shall be by your side. Angel Book 1:18

This extraordinary journal represents compelling evidence that angels are more than abstractions or fable characters; that they are indeed powerful guardians and intercessors who love us more than we could ever comprehend—this side of heaven. What also comes through is how much we need our angels' protection in a world where, as the Lord said through Vassula, "evil is prowling among you like a wolf...." The messages address questions and skepticism very concretely as Vassula's angel and the Lord patiently work through what Vassula has described as her abysmal ignorance of the divine supernatural.

Vassula's awareness of her angel's presence changed everything. How could it not? Still, she struggled a long time with how this could be happening and more so, she wondered, "Why to me?" She could not foresee how this might help others, but has since come to understand that it really is the gift from our Loving Father to all His children. She also understands that He chose her because no one could be more oblivious or indifferent to God than Vassula was at that point in her life. Thus, no one who reads these messages of love is beyond recognizing that not only is our guardian angel always with us, but so is our Blessed Lord.

We would urge you to understand that Vassula is what the Lord called "a sign" of our own angel's presence. If we grasp this, it will be for us, as it was for her, only the beginning of a new awakening. It would lead inevitably to a deeper awareness of God's living presence, of His love for each of us and of why He created us.

The Lord wrote by Vassula's hand in October 1986: Angel Book 2:51-52

> "...I am your Redeemer; I will always be; I will never leave you. I love you...turn to me and look at me; I am God, your Heavenly Father; realize why I am with you; I, God, will do the same thing to all my other sons and daughters, for you are all mine...I, God, love all of you; I am going to reunite you all."

The Publishers
February 1995

viii

Presentation

By Robert J. Carroll

United States Foreign Service Officer, Retired

"I Am Your Guardian Angel and My Name Is Daniel"

With these words, being formed effortlessly and mysteriously by the pencil in her hand on a piece of paper where she had intended to make a shopping list, the life of Vassula Ryden took an unimaginable turn and was changed forever. Looking back on that moment, Vassula herself marvels that she was not shocked and completely unnerved by this phenomenon.

Certainly her inner strength at that point in her life was nothing like what it was to become under the ensuing divine tutelage and tremendous trials that have shaped her since that afternoon in Dhaka, Bangladesh almost nine years ago. But even then, before her gradual but profound spiritual conversion, she accepted with wonder and delight that this was actually happening to her. Her husband, Per Ryden, a Swedish specialist in developmental assistance, had read some mystical theology as a student and hastened to reassure Vassula that such things have indeed happened to mortals before. One of her two sons, with somewhat less theological grounding, exclaimed: "Mom, this is like what happened to Moses!"

Vassula's best friend, Beatrice, a French-Swiss international civil servant who was also living in Dhaka at that time, told me recently that Vassula first confided this experience to her during lunch one day in 1986. "You are going to think I'm crazy," Vassula said, "but I have been receiving messages from my angel." Beatrice didn't know what to think except that she knew Vassula was about as solidly grounded in reality as anyone she had ever known. When Beatrice read Angel Daniel's words to Vassula, her eyes filled with tears. She told Vassula that the tenderness and love in those words left no doubt that they were of divine origin.

When I first heard Vassula tell her story on an audio tape of a talk she gave in Pittsburgh in 1991, I felt joy and a great sense of hope because, although this might have sounded on the face of it highly implausible, I knew from Vassula's straight forward sincerity and the majesty of the messages she was reading, that this was indeed the real thing. The Lord was speaking to us clearly and forcefully when we so desperately need His guidance and encouragement.

At that time, I was an American diplomat serving at the U.S. Embassy in Stockholm, Sweden. These powerful messages spoke right to my heart and I began sharing them with others to the limits of my resources. I was surprised myself at what a far-reaching impact there was in Sweden alone. I have since seen a similar impact throughout the United States and other parts of the world despite some predictable derision and mean-spirited attacks against Vassula.

The fruits I have witnessed have been concrete and unmistakable. So, I am one of many who have been trying to spread awareness of these uplifting words simply because they touch people so powerfully and in a lasting way.

It is noteworthy—although it should go without saying—that no one, including Vassula herself, who has been playing a significant role in spreading these consoling messages, has gained any material enrichment from doing so. Without exception, those who have done the most to further this apostolate of unity and sacred intimacy with Our Creator have reached into their own pockets to do so. I believe that they will continue to make these sacrifices cheerfully because they have been blessed with daily confirmation that these messages are helping those around us and across a broad range of people and nations. These messages offer great hope for all God's children and His creation. We believe, as a highly-respected priest in Connecticut said recently, that "Vassula Ryden is the most important prophet of our time."

This phenomenon, which began through Vassula's angel, has helped so many of us to grasp the reality of God's loving dialogue with His children as recorded throughout the Bible and through the great mystical writers right up to this modern age of unprecedented rationalism. As was recently expressed by Father Michael Kaszowski, a professor at the Katowice Seminary in Poland, authentic private revelations lead to deeper understanding of Scripture and to hunger for God's Word.

I have had the privilege of knowing the writer of the following Introduction, Father Michael O'Carroll, the beloved and highly-acclaimed theologian who has been Vassula's spiritual advisor during the last several years of her extraordinary experience. Father O'Carroll has long been applying his wisdom and learning to validate and illuminate the great mystical traditions of Christianity. Aside from this, he is the sort of man with whom it is enough to be in his kind and gentle presence to feel uplifted. The fact that this theologian and saintly people I have come to know have embraced *True Life in God* wholeheartedly, further confirms in my mind the divine inspiration of these beautiful messages.

Father Michael describes how grateful he was when he only recently came to read Vassula's early dialogue with her angel that preceded the messages of *True Life in God*. Others already following the messages will be powerfully touched all over again as I was when I was given one of these notebooks of holy discourse and began to read how it all began. Having let decades of my life go by, as Vassula did, without giving more than passing thought to any world but this one, I could put myself very readily in Vassula's place. I could identify closely with her reactions as her angel gently revealed to her that the only reality that counts is that of a loving God who knows and cares about each one of us more than we could ever imagine.

As evidenced by the mushrooming readership of books about angels and other apparently heavenly interventions—and as Pope John Paul has said so eloquently in his writings—there is an abiding hunger of the human soul for some degree of intimacy with this personal God. It is a hunger that will not be satisfied with any counterfeit mysticism that dismisses the Un-caused Cause and the Savior of mankind, who truly walked this earth, as merely some mindless force in the universe.

Even the skeptical may recognize these messages to be what some of the holiest and brightest religious scholars of our time consider to be inherently authentic. It is difficult to gauge how the general public will react if this extraordinary book reaches beyond the already spiritually-minded to a wider, more secular audience. Many today profess an indifference to God. These messages might prove to be a basis to begin a friendship with Him. This may be why He chose a person like Vassula who was far from God and felt neither guilt nor emptiness over it. She had after all a full, satisfying life in which she was—as many today have become—too busy for spiritual speculations.

There are also those who are increasingly distressed by the way civilization seems to be tending and blame God for humanity's failings. Early on, Vassula spoke for all of us when she wondered how a loving God could allow such suffering. I found the response she received to be both illuminating and consoling. Perhaps those similarly troubled may discover in the divine revelations to Vassula a loving Father who is bending down from heaven to guide and comfort us and bring His Kingdom to earth by finding a dwelling place in each of our hearts.

The book may also reach those who have been holding out for something beyond the pseudo-spirituality and religiosity that comes at us from all directions and crowds out genuine spirituality and contemplation. A personal God, who not only offers eternal happiness but makes demands on those who respond, has never been universally popular. But here the Lord, through Vassula, is issuing a fresh invitation to those who are disillusioned but who, by better knowing God, might more easily accept Him for the Loving Father that He is. The Lord, in His Divine wisdom, knows how to touch every good heart. When Vassula asked on December 30, 1986: "Lord, are you the same One who called Moses?" she received this response: Angel Book 4:4

> "I am the same God; era O era! little do you know that I, God, shine on every faithful heart, I will always find ways of calling you (He continued in Greek): although the world has abandoned the Light, I, God Almighty, will find a means to shine on you...I, God, love all of you, augment your love for me."

In Vassula's case as with most genuine mystical experiences such as those at Lourdes, France, Fatima and Portugal, an angel precedes the divine revelations. Vassula's unique gift, however, was to be enabled to keep this journal of conversations with her guardian angel and to share it with us. For her it was like the dawning of an entirely new existence. Few of us who read these conversations now will escape this same dramatic impact of knowing that guardian angels do indeed exist and that God has provided one to each of us. This, we learn with Vassula, is an important and serious reality, not some legend or fantasy to delight children. Nor is it merely a frivolous invisible companionship as Vassula first accepted it. Rather, our guardian angel is everything we may have been told as children, but much, much more.

It was a great awakening for Vassula as she began to grasp the meaning of this angelic presence. But the most important thing she came to comprehend was that not only is God's angel always with us but so is God Himself. Vassula wondered why the Lord had chosen this unique, unprecedented means of communicating His message: His living presence actually manifested in the handwriting. This was His response on November 18, 1986: Angel Book 3:20-21

> *"...by calling you in this way I mean to conduct others too, for all those who abandoned Me and do not hear Me; because of these reasons this call is in written form; I, Yahweh, will remind them in this call of many events so that My beloved ones may approach Me; accept the way I am conducting you: I will encourage those with little faith to build up their faith in Me; it is a call for those who laid aside My Word, to bring them back and read My Word; it is to tell them that My Word is Alive, Holy and Blessed; it is a call to wake them up; it is a call of love and peace; it is a call to remind them how their foundations began and that I, God, am their Creator; I want to remind them that they are not fatherless and that I love them all..."*

Vassula also was given to understand that this body of messages constitute a "love letter" to each of us. Thus the personal touch of giving them in handwritten form is fitting. Whatever the form, these writings will touch many hearts and souls, including those who might have otherwise considered themselves beyond the reach of a personal brush with the divine supernatural. The Lord tells Vassula that when we read His messages, we should take her name away and replace it with our own, because He is actually speaking to each one of us. It is indeed crucial to take in the Lord's messages in this direct, personal way, rather than reading them as merely observers of Vassula's experience. For those who may have been groping in confusion and darkness, this could be for them the dawning of a bright new day as it was for Vassula.

At whatever point readers may be on their spiritual journey, these messages can be a concrete expression of the great love the Lord has for every one of us. Many will want more of the gentle love, wisdom and truth they sample in the angel dialogue and, if they are willing, their hearts will be gently drawn into a union of true peace, love and joy and—most assuredly—a deeper meaning of existence in discovering a True Life in God. For each of you who do this there will be another angel as joyful as was Vassula's Angel Daniel.

Vassula with Her Angel Daniel

Introduction
by Father Michael O'Carroll, C.S.Sp.
Vassula's Spiritual Advisor

Vassula's Initiation

Those who have heard Vassula Ryden speak about her unique experience and those who have read about it know that a long period of divine teaching and formation took place before she received the messages contained in the series of books titled *True Life In God*. Up until now, we have only heard brief summaries of what transpired between November 1985 and the first published message of September 20, 1986 ("Peace be with you"). Now, by the grace of God, the present book brings to light the gentle yet powerful conversations of that early period. They provide for us a case history of an initiation to a prolonged mystical experience that to my knowledge is unparalleled in the history of such things.

In the midst of writing a third book on Vassula's messages and mission, I am delighted to have this dialogue now. It affords firsthand documentation on the divine pedagogy under which she advanced to fulfill her vocation. I am also grateful to witness in these writings the successive entry into her life, into her spiritual experience, of each Divine Person, Father, Son and Holy Spirit. My book is entitled *Vassula, Apostle of the Holy Trinity*.

Vassula Ryden's initiation was undertaken and accomplished by her Guardian Angel. Listeners to Vassula on five continents have heard that her very first experience of a supernatural intervention in her life was a message from her Guardian Angel identifying himself as "Daniel." What happened thereafter? How exactly did this extraordinary initiation and formation unfold from then onward? The record here faithfully set down will not only answer these questions; it will reassure anyone that has been exposed to the theological skeptics of our age, those who cast doubt upon the very existence of angels, possibly making fun of those of us who have long believed in our guardian angels.

Angels are everywhere these days, in bookstores, gift shops, on record albums—even in movies about baseball, I am told. Hence arises the question: are they real? Must we believe in them? Here I think I should give the answer offered by a great French theologian: who am I to oppose the observations of those who wrote the books of the Bible—Old and New Testament, of the Fathers of the Church, the first great exponents of the riches of our faith; of all the great theologians of the Church—East and West—right down to our own time? St. Thomas Aquinas in his great *Summa Theological* devoted 15 questions and answers to the angels—their nature, their creation, their mission and ministry. He discusses specifically the question of guardian angels (Question 113). From the moment of birth an angel is assigned to every human being without exception.

Of course I believe in angels. They complete the Christian concept of the world. Between humankind—which is spirit and matter—and God, the Infinite One, pure Spirit, One in Three. Angels are pure spirits—created and finite. This makes a wonderful cosmic entity: creation rising in beautiful tiers to meet the Source of all things, God the Creator. On reflection, given the nearly infinite number and levels in the order of living things between the single cell and human beings in this visible world, would it seem likely that there would be no other beings between human souls and Almighty God in the spiritual realm?

Devout Catholics, including saints, have had an elevating belief and relationship centered on the Guardian Angel, one of the heavenly host assigned to assist, protect and eventually escort to glory each individual. Our angel transmits the Holy Spirit's gifts to us and takes our prayers, enhances them and presents them to the Triune God. This spiritual reality is another example of divine love, generosity and care for every one of us. It is a reality to cherish and to live with. It is a reality which we should not neglect.

The dialogue between Vassula and her angel is typically Christian, a blend of the mysterious and transcendental with what is natural and simple: as for example when she asks "Where are you usually?" and receives the reply, "I am where you are." Or again, "Where will you be when I die?" "You will meet me; I shall be by your side." Meanwhile, we hear about the "snake," but this is an occasion to offer encouragement. Note the words, "I will defend you; I will guard you and give you every protection; you need never fear." In passing, I remind the reader that the words "Be not afraid" are found over 250 times in the Bible. As readers of *True Life In God* know, the Bible is evoked throughout the communications of Jesus to Vassula. The angel saw to her readiness for these messages from the beginning: "Read the Bible every day and your soul shall progress."

There is a frankness, at times surprising, in the dialogue between Vassula and her angel. She speaks more to her supernatural visitor at this stage than later when it is Jesus or the Father or the Holy Spirit who comes to enlighten her and—through her—all those who enter into communion with the messages and the One who gives them. The spiritual drama continues as the angel gradually gives way to Jesus and the Father in this series of spiritual encounters.

We get insight too into the problem of spiritual guidance with which Vassula had to grapple. She was totally ignorant of mystical theology and unaware even of the possibility of supernatural interventions in human life. Yet she dreaded consultations with the very people who would be presumed to have the required knowledge and background; she had to remain suspicious of the only people from whom she might seek assistance.

It would be utterly impossible for Vassula to have come through this initial testing phase on her own. She would have succumbed to the adversary, whose presence was on occasion palpable. As to her capacity to invent this entire spiritual saga, it was—and I say this with the fullest sense of responsibility—totally nil. If it had not happened, there was no way whatever that she could have invented it. The nature of the dialogue, including her questioning and resistance make this point beyond reasonable doubt.

The dialogue with the Father in which all of this unfolds is exciting reading. What stands out is how the Father, in a highly personal way, offers His first revelation; I almost said His self-portrait. This is very precious at the present time.

The note of divine choice of predestination is strong in these pages, and with what a sense of inexhaustible goodness and mercy!

One meets the mighty One, Creator and Sovereign Lord of all things. The style of language is at times particularly reminiscent of the Old Testament:

> "I am Yahweh, your Creator and you are my children; where, where do you think you will go? Did you really believe you just came on your own? Had you believed that I had left you? Or that I never existed? My Word is alive and the Truth; it is to enlighten you and help you understand who I am, what you are; My Word is to help you find Me...I, God, am your Creator; I have created you because I love life...I created the heavens; I created everything; how else did you think all this was done?...let your academies...find the answer to the vital question: why do you exist?...some of you do not even bother to ask any questions, accepting life as it comes, not believing that your soul keeps on living once you die; blind! blind! and deaf! refusing to see and hear; are you afraid of finding the truth? I am the Truth...are you searching? I am the Way...I am the Way and I love you; I am the Light that shines for everyone to see the Truth; beloved children, My Heart pains to see you all sleeping; how could I not come to you and warn you? how could I leave you when evil is prowling among you like a wolf waiting to devour you? I want to wake you up so that you meet Me." Angel Book 2:16-18.

As the sacred communication progresses there is perceptible change as Vassula grows in faith, knowledge and love of God. Her need to seek reassurance lessens, she grows more comfortable in this unusual role, which in turn allows fuller statements from her divine visitor.

Those who have already been helped by reading the previous volumes of *True Life in God* will be further enlightened, encouraged and strengthened by this book. Those who have so far been unaware of this tremendous gift from heaven will have an opportunity to respond to the invitation issued by Our Lord in the message of November 17, 1986: Angel Book 3:17-18

> "Lift your eyes and look at the One who adopts you now; understand that I, it is, who gave you this gift; yes, I have blessed you and gave you My Peace; beloved, you are Mine; learn how

I, Yahweh work; learn by reading My Word; I am your Teacher so do not despair, for you are at the beginning of your learning...do not be afraid...come to Me any time for I am your Redeemer..."

Me and you bless God bless God

Vassula with Her Angel Daniel

Foreword
by Vassula Ryden

The Approach of My Angel

In the beginning one of the first things my guardian angel put on paper was a drawing of a heart; from the centre of the heart he drew a rose as though it was growing out from the heart. Then gently and still to my great astonishment he introduced himself as my guardian angel, Daniel. He left me bewildered but with great joy at the same time. I was so happy that I was almost flying around the house, my feet barely touching the ground and I was repeating loudly: "I am the luckiest person on earth, and I am probably the only person on earth who could communicate in such a way with her angel!"

The following day my angel returned to me as before. I spent endless joyful hours communicating with him. Again, the next day he returned, but this time, to my great surprise, he brought with him a multitude of angels of different choirs. I felt that the gates of heaven were suddenly wide open because I could easily sense this great movement of angels from above. They all appeared excited and happy, just like when someone is expecting something wonderful to happen. From the way they rejoiced, I understood that heaven was having a feast and they were celebrating. Then, the angels all together sang in one voice these words: "A happy event is about to come!" I knew that whatever that event would be, it concerned me directly, but, although I tried hard to guess, I could not tell what it was. This chorus was sung all day long, with the same words and only a few minutes of silence in between this chorus. Every time heaven opened, the angels repeated the same chorus.

The first words my angel pronounced about God were the following: "God is near you and loves you."

I must have wounded the Lord very much this minute, because His words had no effect on me whatsoever. When my angel pronounced these words about God, I remember that I thought it was a normal thing for an angel to say, since angels lived near God. I did not reply and my angel did not add anything more.

Only a few days later, my angel suddenly changed attitude with me and I noticed how very grave he became. In a very solemn voice he asked me to read The Word. I pretended I did not know what The Word meant and asked him the meaning of it. With this, my angel became even more grave telling me that I knew very well what he meant, nevertheless, he told me that it was the Holy Bible. I already had my answer on my tongue and told him I did not have one at home. He said that he knew that I did not have one. He asked me to go and fetch one. Arguing still with him, I said that he was asking me the impossible, because in a Moslem country in which I lived then, (Bangladesh), the book stores did not sell Bibles. He said that I should go immediately to the American School, where my son went, and fetch one from their library. I was debating whether to go or simply stay at home and refuse. The other thing that was embarrassing me was how would my husband and all my friends react to all this. I simply could not see myself standing in front of them with a Bible! Already I was thinking of places in the house where I would hide it, were I to bring one home. But seeing again the grave look on my angel's face I decided to obey him. So I went to the school and saw several Bibles on the shelves. I chose one and brought it home. I opened it to read, just as my angel had asked me to do. My eyes fell on the psalms: I read, but could not understand a single word. This was a sign from God, showing me how blind I was.

The Purification

My angel came back to me still very grave and reproached me for certain acts I had done in my lifetime that displeased God very much. Then he reproached me of how I had thrown at God's Face His gifts, gifts that He had given me but that I had not appreciated at all.

With this he started to remind me and show me the sins I had never confessed. He showed them to me as on a screen. He reminded me of the event and of how much it offended God. But the most severe reproaches I received were about the rejection of God's gifts. My angel told me that it was a great offence to God to deny and throw away His gifts. He made me see my sins with the eyes of God, the way God sees them and not the way we see them. They were so monstrous that I despised myself while weeping bitterly. This state

I was put in was, I understood later on, a grace from God so that I would repent sincerely. I was shown my sins so crystal clear, exposing the interior of my soul so openly, that it was as if I was turned inside out. I suddenly realized how Adam and Eve must have felt after they had sinned, when God approached them in His Light, facing them. My soul was uncovered and at display; it felt naked, loathsome and ugly. I could only tell my angel between my sobs that I do not deserve a decent death, and that being like I am, so utterly wicked, I should die and be cut into small pieces and thrown away to the hyenas.

This purification must have gone on for almost a week. It felt like fire, a cleansing fire purifying the interior of my soul, and it was a very painful experience indeed.

The Our Father Taught by Our Creator

After this experience that had left me shattered, God our Eternal Father revealed Himself to me. I did not see Him with the eyes of my soul, as I used to see my angel, but I knew it was Him and heard Him. I remember that my reaction was one like, "Ah, it is God and He can help us now!" This is why He asked me, "Do you really believe I can help you?" And I answered Him, "Yes!" then I remember going near the window saying to Him, "Look! Look how the world has become!" I wanted to show Him how the world had become. God did not comment but asked me to pray to Him the Our Father. I prayed to Him the Our Father while He was with me, listening, and when I finished He said that He was not pleased with the way I said it because I prayed it too fast. So I repeated it all over again to Him but slower. Again He told me that He was not pleased because I was moving. He asked me to pray it again. I prayed it again and in the end God said that it was not satisfying Him still. I prayed it several times but every time He said He was not pleased. I started to wonder, I started to wonder whether He was making me pray all the Our Fathers that I had not been praying all these years in one single day! I had started in the morning and now it was night. Suddenly He was satisfied, for every sentence I pronounced, He said, "Good!", with delight. I will try to give an example to explain what really happened:

If you were visited one day by a relative you had never met before because he lived in another country; in the beginning of your encounter you might tend to feel distant to him and maybe formal. But the more time would go by during that day you would seem to feel closer to him than in the very beginning, and so by the end of that day you would notice that a sympathy developed in you that was not there before.

And this is how it was with my first encounter with God. When I was praying the Our Father, to God, in the beginning I was distant, but His visit which lasted the whole day changed me because when I was saying this prayer to Him, I was enjoying His presence and the words I was telling Him took some meaning. He was so fatherly, very tender and very warm. The intonation of His Voice was making me feel so much at ease, that somehow, during that day, instead of responding, "Yes Lord," I found myself saying, "Yes, Dad." I had later on apologized to God for saying, "Dad," but He said that He had taken that word like a jewel. He seemed so very pleased. And that is how finally I realized that God had feelings and that He wanted me to tell Him this prayer with MY HEART.

Satan's Assaults

Before I come into this paragraph I would like to write what Father Marie-Eugene says in his book, "I am a Daughter of the Church," about demoniac attacks.

> "What is at stake in this encounter between the human and the divine, the purity of God and the soul's impurity, is too important for the devil not to intervene in it with all the power at his disposal. Yet a little while and the soul purified by the dark night will be secure against his attacks and will be to him a terrible thing. Hence the devil makes use of the advantages he still possesses over it because of its imperfections and its attachments to the sensible. Saint John of the Cross notes that 'the evil one takes his stand, with great cunning, on the road which leads from sense to spirit.'" (Living Flame, st.iii; Peers, III, 83)

> "The darkness of these regions, the soul's disarray, disconcerted as it is by the newness of its experiences and

the intensity of its suffering, create conditions particularly favourable to the interventions of the prince of darkness and of lies."

"By certain exterior signs of calm and of deep silence in the senses, the devil easily guesses that the soul is receiving divine communications. Our mystical doctor says:

> 'Of those favours which come through a good angel God habitually allows the enemy to have knowledge: partly so that he may do that which he can against them according to the measure of justice, and that thus he may not be able to allege with truth that no opportunity is given him for conquering the soul, as he said concerning Job.'
> (Dark Night, Bk. II, xxiii; Peers, I, 449)

"Such are the facts in the problem of the dark night of the spirit, and the causes that produce it. This night is an encounter, or rather a real combat, organized by loving Wisdom. God establishes His perfect reign in the soul only after taking away its unfitness for the divine and conquering all the forces of evil that have any power over it."

This was so that the reader would understand better why God allows Satan to intervene.

Just after this delightful day I had spent with our Father in Heaven, all the fury of hell broke out! In a very savage way Satan attacked me. The first thing I heard from him sounded more like the growl of a wild animal than a voice. That growl seemed to say, "GOOOO!" I guessed that "Go" meant that I should stop having communications with my angel and with God. All distressed I turned around in search of my angel, but Satan seemed to have taken all the space and with great hatred began to call me all sorts of names. He produced such anguish and such terror in my soul that I could have died had it not been that God had a plan for me. I never sensed such fury before. I ordered him to go away and this seemed to raise his fury even more. It was like the fury of a madman. Fuming with rage and like someone out of his mind he growled, his voice was very hoarse when he said: "EH? withdraw from here you b..., withdraw, or else, fire in hell does the rest!" I heard myself answering him: "No!" With my "No" I meant that I will NOT LEAVE the presence of God nor my angel. Then he snapped back that I was cursed and called me all sorts of dirty names.

It is difficult to explain this anguish the devil can infuse in the soul. This phenomenon that occurs is something that although your logic tells you you're not mad, you yourself yet cannot control. This anguish used to come in waves, as if Satan himself were not enough, he sent other demons too to attack me. When they used to attack me it was something frightening growing within me, nothing to do with exterior fear. It was a feeling I was unable to push away.

My poor angel, in these terrible moments, moments that made me believe sometimes I would lose my mind, could only tell me one word, "PRAY!" I prayed and begged my angel to help me come out of this experience, for it seemed to last forever.

The Battle Between My Angel and Satan

As though it was not enough to be tormented in the daytime, Satan came too at nighttime. He would not let me sleep. Every time I was about to fall asleep, he would try to suffocate me. I sometimes would feel him like an eagle who would put his claws inside my stomach, and squeeze all the breath out of me. I felt the battle around me, I felt how I was in the middle of this battle, between my angel and the devil. Then one day, as if nothing had happened, everything ceased. Satan abandoned his attacks and I had a few days peace. All this experience left me rather weak, but more attached than ever before to my angel.

In my eyes my guardian angel began to be everything, and he filled my life. I clung to him for dear life so to say. I realized how much our guardian angels protected us, loved us, cared for us, guarded us, cried for us, prayed for us, suffered with us and shared everything with us. Sorrows and joys were shared.

To the horror of the devil, since he guessed what God had in store for me, he came back into the scene. Cunning as he is, this time he changed strategy. He used the classical way to deceive me and appeared to me like my angel. He attached a great importance on how to portray God to me. His aim, since he guessed that God would approach me for a mission, was to make me fear God in the wrong way, so that when God's time came to communicate with me, I would run away from Him.

I admit that in the beginning he managed to deceive me and I believed what he said about God, because he used my ignorance to feed my brain with a false image of God. He portrayed God to me as a fearful judge, with little tolerance for His creatures, and that with the slightest error on our part, He would punish us in a terrible way. This went on for a few days.

I came to the stage where I could not discern who was who. I could not tell if I was with my angel or if it was the evil one aping my angel. I had nobody to turn to for consulting or take advice from either. I was quite alone. I also did not want to share this with my husband, for fear of upsetting him. Satan believing he had now the upper hand, started to tighten the knot, by showing signs of evil, wickedness, confusing me. To make things worse, every day that went by, he brought more and more demons with him, to invade me, making it very difficult for my guardian angel to protect me. God allowed me to overhear the devil once, while he was giving orders to his angels to go and attack and paralyse me. These fallen angels surrounded me, mocked me, lied to me and called me all sorts of dirty names. They also nick-named me "Pia" but with mockery. God allowed all this to happen, for this too was another way that He made use of, to purify my soul.

My Purification Continues

A few days passed and suddenly my angel asked me to go to the seminary to find a priest and show him the messages. I did exactly as he told me. But I was very disappointed. I had great expectations and what I got was a blow. The priest thought I was going through a psychological crisis and believed I was on the verge of schizophrenia. He wanted to examine both my hands. He took both my hands and analyzed them. I knew what he had in mind, he was trying to find traces of any sort of abnormality in my hands as in certain mental cases. He believed that now God had given him this heavy cross, that was me, to carry. He pitied me and asked me to come any time to see him. I went every second or third day to visit him. I did not like going to him because he treated me as a mental case in the beginning. This went on for about three or four months. The only reason why I persevered in visiting him was so that I should prove to him I was not mental. Finally after some time he realized that I was sane. One day he even said that what I had might be a charisma from God.

My guardian angel in the meantime was leading me towards God and one of the first lessons that he gave me was on discernment. These teachings on discernment infuriated the devil even more because it meant that even though he would appear like the angel of light, I would know the difference.

My angel told me that Jesus will approach me and that his mission (my angel's) was coming towards its end. When I heard this news I was sad. I did not want my angel to leave me. He tried to reason with me explaining that he was only God's servant and that now I should turn towards God. He tried to explain that his mission with me was to take me to God and hand me safely over to Him. But this was all the more painful for me. I could not bear the idea that from one day to the other I would not communicate with my angel.

As my angel Daniel foretold to me, one day Jesus came in his place. When He revealed Himself to me, He asked me, "Which house is more important, your house or My House?" I answered Him, "Your House." I felt Him happy with my reply, He blessed me and left.

Again, instead of my angel, the Lord came to me, and said, "It is I," and when He saw I was hesitating, He said clearly, "It is I, God." But instead of rejoicing I was unhappy. I was missing terribly my angel. I loved my angel deeply and the mere thought that he would not come again because his place would be taken by God was disturbing me. I would like to mention here, what the Lord told me regarding the love I had for my angel. He said that no one ever loved his angel as much as I have, and He hoped to say one day to me these words: "No man ever loved Me in your era as much as you have."

Now my angel kept in the background. God asked me, "Do you love Me?" I said I did. He did not blame me for not loving Him enough, but instead He said very gently, "Love Me more."

The other time the Lord revealed Himself to me He told me, "Revive My House," and again, "Renew My House." I could not remember replying, but I knew that what He was asking me was impossible.

The following days were visits either by my angel or Jesus, sometimes both at the same time. My angel was preaching to me, he was asking me to make peace with God. When he asked me that, I was very surprised, and I told him that I was not at war with God, so how was I to make peace with Him?

God asked me again to love Him. He asked me to become intimate with Him as I was with my angel, meaning to speak freely to Him, but I could not. I still felt Him as a stranger and not as a friend. My angel was reminding me that he was just God's servant and that I should love God and glorify Him. The more he was pushing me towards God, the more I was panicking for fear that he would leave me. He was telling me to abandon myself to God, but I was not doing it.

Meanwhile Satan had not given up, he still hoped to get me in my weak state. I was allowed by God once or twice to hear a conversation between Jesus and Satan. Satan was asking from Him to put me to the test. He said to Jesus: "We will see about your Vassula...your dear Vassula will not keep faithful to You, she will fall and for good this time, I can prove it to You in the days of her trials." And so Satan was allowed again to place on me all sorts of temptations. Incredible temptations! Every time I realized that it was a temptation and I overcame it, he put in my way yet another bigger temptation. Temptations that had I succumbed to them, my soul would be bound for hell. Then his attacks started all over again. He splashed boiling oil on my mid-finger where I place the pencil to write. Immediately the blister appeared and I had to dress it to be able to hold the pencil when I was writing. The devil was trying once more and ever so hard to stop me from communicating with God and from writing. I wrote with great pain. Each time my finger healed, he repeated the same thing over and over again, and so for weeks I wrote, but not without suffering.

When my family and I went on a holiday to Thailand, we went in a boat to visit an island. On the way back as soon as we were pulling in, the boat shook and I lost my balance. So that I do not fall I grabbed the first thing in sight and it was the exhaust pipe of the boat, burning hot. I burned the whole palm of my right hand. My first thought was "How am I to write?" My hand swelled, was red and very painful. We were half an hour from the hotel but by the time we arrived there all the swelling and pain had left me. I had no sign of burning. The Lord told me later on that He had not allowed Satan to go as far as this, and so He healed my hand.

The devil tried another way to stop me from writing. He appeared to my son, (he was ten years old then), in his dream. He took the shape of an old man and told him while sitting near his bed, "You'd better tell your mother to stop writing, and if she does not, I shall do to you the same thing I had done to her when she was young. I shall come while you are lying in bed, pull your head back and strangle you."

This was what I experienced when I was maybe six years old. I had seen one night right in front of me, while I was in bed, just above my throat, two terribly ugly hands of an old man. The next thing I knew was that something pulled my head backwards, exposing my throat. Then nothing. But this left me trembling.

Satan had hounded me from my early age, for almost every night at about the age of six, he appeared to me in dreams to terrify me, taking the shape of a big black dog. It was always the same dream. I would be walking in a dimmed corridor and there at the end would be this dog snarling, ready to jump on me and tear me to pieces, and I would flee terrified.

When I was about 10, I saw Jesus in my dream. He was at the end of some sort of corridor. I only saw His portrait. I saw Him only all the way to His waist. He was smiling and saying, "Come, come to Me." I was suddenly seized by an unknown current that drew me closer and closer to Him. I was afraid of this unknown current and Jesus realized my fear, smiling at me. This current drew me all the way to Jesus until my face stuck on His face.

At about twelve years of age too, I had another mystical experience. It was my spiritual marriage to Jesus. Again in a dream, I was dressed as a bride and my spouse was Jesus. Only I could not see

Him but I knew He was there. The people who were present were greeting us cheerfully with palm leaves in their hands. We were supposed to walk the nuptial walk. Just after the marriage was over, I stepped in a room. There was our Blessed Mother with St. Mary Magdalene and two other holy women. Our Blessed Mother was very happy and came to embrace me. She started immediately to fix my dress again and my hair and I realized that She wanted me to be presentable for Her Son.

Satan Continues with Different Attacks

The devil knew what a horror I have for cockroaches. I hate to write this, but I feel I must, to show how the devil fought me. One day while going out of a room, I shut the door. I suddenly felt on my face a wet liquid that was sprinkled on me. I could not understand where it came from. I heard suddenly Satan laughing and he mockingly said to me: "This is the way I baptize. This is the kind of holy water you deserve!" Then I saw what had happened. I had squashed at the frame of the door a big cockroach...I could have died there and then from my disgust! I do not like writing so much about Satan's attacks, but I would like to show how much he fought me to prevent this message from coming out and prevent me from the mission the Lord was preparing for me.

One day he decided again to change strategy. To deceive me, he took the exact image of my deceased father. Even the manner he spoke to me was the same. A perfect imitation. He spoke to me in French as my father now and then did and said: "My dear, look...God, out of pity is sending me to you to tell you that you are wrong. How could you believe that He communicates with you in this way? These things are, as you know, impossible, and you are only offending and angering God. Think...God speaking to you? Where did you ever hear of such a thing before? Only madness can lead you to believe such a thing!" I asked, "Well what about my angel, with angels is it possible?" When he said, "Oh that one..." his voice was filled with hatred and I recognized Satan once more.

The Desert, Then the Total Surrender

That is why I am going to seduce her and lead her out into the wilderness and speak to her heart. (Ho 2:16)

Now God wanted me to surrender fully to Him. He wanted to unite me to Him and make me His. He wanted to mould me and transform me. I was not surrendering according to His desire and so I had to undergo another sort of purification for my total abandonment to God so that I make peace with Him. This is what happened: I called to God and to my surprise I had no response. I panicked and turned around to look for my angel, but he was not there either. Instead, I felt a few souls around me, they came like beggars, approaching me.[1] They begged me for prayers, blessings and for holy water. I went to the church immediately and brought with me holy water for them. They asked me to sprinkle it on them and so I did. This gesture attracted even more souls and in no time I had around me a big crowd. To my surprise it seemed to relieve them from their pains and their joy was great. One of them asked me to pray for him there and then and give him just one blessing. I did not know how, so he told me to just pray a simple prayer and bless him. I prayed as he asked me and blessed him. He thanked me with joy and he himself blessed me too. All this was new to me, but I felt that they were relieved and pleased. I took the opportunity to ask them whether they knew where my angel was, the one whom my heart already had begun to love. But I did not get any answer.

Every day that went by in this loneliness seemed like a year. I was looking for peace and I could not find it. I was surrounded by many friends and people but I never felt so lonely and abandoned as that time. I felt as though I was going through hell. Many a time I cried out for my angel to return to me, but no, he had vanished! My soul failed at his flight. I sought him but I did not find him, I called to him but he did not answer. I roamed for three whole weeks in the desert, more dead than alive, until I could not bear it any longer and in this terrible night that my soul was going through I cried out tearfully

---

1. When I was a teenager, I used to see with the eyes of my soul many souls surrounding me. When I saw these souls then, I would say to myself, "Ah, again here are the dead people." They filled the room I was in. They seemed to sit close to each other on the floor. I felt they enjoyed my presence. All of them seemed alike. They appeared thin with no hair and grayish in their looks. Their whole self was grayish like ash. They did not make any sound and in fact they seemed like they did not want to disrupt me. This was a very common scene that occurred for several years. Later on, Jesus explained all this to me. He said that these souls were waiting for my prayers when I would be converted.

with all my heart and as never before to Yahweh: "FA-THER!!...where are You?...Father?...Why did You leave me? O God, take me! Take me and use me as You wish!...Purify me so that You are able to use me!"

With this piercing cry that came from the depths of my heart, heaven suddenly opened and like thunder the Father's voice, full of emotion cried back to me: "I GOD LOVE YOU!" These words were like a balm pouring on those impressive wounds my soul received and they healed me instantly. I felt in those words uttered by God His Infinite Love.

Just after these words of love, it seemed to me as though I dropped out of a tornado into a beautiful peaceful garden. My angel reappeared and with great tenderness began to dress my wounds, those wounds I received while crossing by night this endless desert.

Yahweh then asked me to open the Bible and read. The first passage I read brought me to tears and converted me, for it revealed to me in an amazing way the Heart of God. I read in Exodus 22:25, 26 these words:

> "If you take another's cloak as a pledge, you must give it back to him before sunset. It is all the covering he has; it is the cloak he wraps his body in; what else would he sleep in? If he cries to me, I will listen, for I am full of pity."

God did not explain to me immediately what happened in these three weeks for His own reasons but much later, on December 22, 1990, He gave me this explanation, here are His own words:

> "...My Heart, an Abyss of Love, cried out for you. You had accumulated sorrow upon sorrow in My Heart, treason upon treason. You were wrestling with Me, puny little creature...but I knew that your heart is not a divided heart and that once I conquered your heart, it would become entirely Mine. An object of your era, you were wrestling with Me, but I have thrown you down in the battle and dragged you in the dust and into the desert where I left you there all alone. I had provided you with a guardian angel, since the beginning of your existence, to guard you, console you and guide you. But My Wisdom ordered your

guardian angel to leave you and to let you face the desert on your own. I said: 'You are to live in spite of your nakedness!'[1] Because no man is able to survive alone,[2] Satan would have taken over completely and would have killed you. My order was given to him too. I forbade him to touch you. Then in your terror you remembered Me and looked up in heaven searching desperately for Me. Your laments and your supplications suddenly broke the deathly stillness surrounding you and your terrified cries pierced through the heavens reaching the Holy Trinity's Ears...'My child!' The Father's voice full of joy resounded through all heaven. 'Ah...I shall now make her penetrate My Wounds[3] and let her eat My Body and drink My Blood. I shall espouse her to Me and she will be Mine for eternity. I shall show her the Love I have for her and her lips from thereon shall thirst for Me and her heart shall be My headrest. She shall eagerly submit daily to My Righteousness, and I shall make her an alter of My Love and of My Passion. I, and I only shall be her only love and passion, and I shall send her with My Message to the ends of the world to conquer an irreligious people and to a people who are not even her own. And voluntarily she will carry My Cross of Peace and Love taking the road to Calvary.' 'And I, the Holy Spirit shall descend upon her to reveal to her the Truth and the depths of Us.[4] I shall remind the world through her that the greatest of all the gifts is: LOVE.' 'Let Us then celebrate! Let all heaven celebrate!'"

God gave me a vision to better understand the situation. He made me understand why Satan was so aggressive with me. So long as I was not fully converted, the devil did not disturb me and felt content. He did not show any aggression. But the moment he felt I was turning towards God, and he would lose me, he attacked my soul.

1. I became "naked" as soon as my guardian angel and all Heaven had turned their back to me.
2. Abandoned by Heaven
3. the Son then spoke
4. the Holy Trinity

This was the vision: I saw myself standing in a room and I saw a snake (Satan) crawling. Apparently that snake was my pet. But as I had lost interest in it, I stopped feeding it. Hungry and astonished it came out of its hole to look for food. I watched it going towards its dish and there it found a couple of grapes. The snake swallowed them but it did not seem satisfied. So it crawled towards the kitchen in search of food. In the meantime, it started to sense that I had changed my feeling towards it and that now I had become its enemy instead of its friend. Because of that, I knew it would try to kill me. I feared, but just then, my guardian angel appeared asking me if I had any problem. I told him about the snake. He told me that he would take care of it. I hesitated whether I should join in the battle or not, and I decided that I should join my angel and do the work together. My angel took a broom and opened a door which led outside, then went to the snake and frightened it away. He then slammed the door shut and we watched from the window how the snake reacted. It panicked. We saw it heading back again towards the door. But the door was safely shut. It went speeding down the staircase and out into the street. The minute it slithered out, it transformed into a huge ugly toad and again into an evil spirit. The alarm was given and the people out there caught it and tied it up.

The Priest Condemns the Messages

I had been going regularly to the seminary to meet with the priest. One day he asked me to see this phenomenon when I was communicating with heaven, and when my communication started, he came over to me and touched my hand to see if he could stop me. He immediately felt a sort of tingling current penetrating into his arm. He did not tell me anything, but later on, since this electric feeling still was with him all afternoon, he went to tell another priest in the seminary what he experienced. The other priest knew about me. When he told him of the incident, he classified it as diabolical rather than Divine and asked him to bring me to him.

He sprinkled his room with holy water, the chair I was to sit on, the desk, the paper and the pencil he would let me use. I went there and he asked me to call "whatever" I was communicating with and ask "it" to write "Glory be to the Father, to the Son and to the Holy

Spirit." I prayed and asked God to write this for me. And He did, but with such power that the pencil broke and I had to complete it with a pen. The priest was furious and also very frightened. He started to tell me all about Satanism, evil, magic, and dumb spirits and that the spirit I was communicating with was not Divine, but a dumb spirit. He filled my head with terror. When I got up to leave he said that I should not come anymore to the seminary and the church unless I stopped writing, at least for some time; and that I should also leave alone the other priest. He gave me three prayers to recite daily, (Saint Michael's, the Memorare of Saint Bernard, and a novena to the Sacred Heart of Jesus). He also gave me a rosary in my hand.

Shattered, I went to the first priest who, at least, was more gentle and I told him what happened. I said that he did not like me visiting him, and that these visits should stop. He looked down, bent his head on one side and did not answer. With this I knew he agreed. I clearly saw and understood that by not visiting him, he would be relieved instantly from a huge cross. I knew I was a persona non grata, so I got up and cried out to him: "You will never see me again in your premises, not until I feel welcomed!" And so I left, thinking I was leaving the Catholic premises for good.

I went back home and wept my eyes out. My angel came to console me, caressing my brow. I lamented to God, "I am confused and my soul is grieving beyond anyone's imagination. I do not know any-more. You say it is You and my heart feels and knows it is You, but he says it is the devil. If it is You, then I want this priest to say and admit one day that my communications are Divine, and I will believe! God simply said, "I will bend him...."

The angel was very tender with me. He dressed my spiritual wounds very gently. I prayed every day the prayers the priest gave me and did exactly what he asked me to do. I stopped using the charism God had given me and I avoided writing.

Since I was living in a Moslem country, I bought a Koran to study and compare it with our Holy Bible. One day when I was taking notes, to my surprise our Heavenly Father approached me. His mere presence filled me with an inexplicable joy and He said to me: "I God love you, daughter, remember always this. Yahweh is My Name."

And while I was holding the pencil, He used my hand to write it on my note paper. A little later on, He descended near me and again He came and said, while using my hand: "I God love you. Vassula, remember always this. I it is who am guiding you. Yahweh is My Name." This was so touching that I broke into tears. I was like a prisoner, forbidden to talk to my Father, forbidden to have any sort of communications with heaven, forbidden to use the charism that God Himself had given me, and forbidden to use this way to approach My Father in heaven. In all these prohibitions, who comes to visit me in "prison"? The One who loves me most! The most Tender Father, the One who holds the whole universe in the palm of His Hand, to show me His affection and His love.

Persecutions from the Priest

The priest, though, did not give up. He wrote letters to me to tell me that all that I had was a mass of rubbish and that I should just look at myself and understand that such a grace would never be given to me. Previously he said such graces were for people who worked for God, similar to Mother Teresa or the like, and with a gesture of his hand, showed me his books on the shelves. Then he tried to frighten me saying it was diabolical, so that I would abandon the writings. He partly managed, for every time after that, when God approached me, I chased Him away. I could barely accept my angel. If I heard from God these words "I, Yahweh love you," I would pretend I heard nothing and would not allow this to be written. If Jesus approached me and told me, "Peace My child" I would turn away from Him and chase Him away, taking Him for the evil one. The priest managed to put in my head that God cannot communicate with a person like me because God goes only to saintly people. I would sometimes become quite aggressive when Jesus would come and speak to me, thinking it was the devil. I would fiercely chase Him away, over and over again.

In the end Wisdom found a way. My angel came telling me that he had a message from Jesus and would tell it to me. He became the go-between. This was a way I could accept, but not always, for I still was under the influence of the priests' words. How and why would the Holy One's Eyes turn and look at a contemptible soul such as mine, let alone speak to me! How could I have believed that God, the Almighty, would speak and communicate in such a simple way with me! In my life I had never heard this. Yes, only in the Holy Bible, with people like Moses, Abraham and the prophets, but this was another story and other times. A fairy-tale, that's what it was, an illusion, my mind reeled because I knew it was happening and I was not mad! Slowly and with time only, these wounds I received from the priests started to heal.

My angel gave me so much peace, preaching to me every single day for hours. Now and then he would leave space for Jesus to quote His Divine words. The first time this happened, I was about to erase the words, since I had allowed myself to write them down. The angel intervened asking me to understand and leave these words since they were truly from Jesus. The words were, "I, Jesus, love you." These were the first written words from Jesus after the crisis. They were written on the 20th of June 1986. Slowly, slowly, step by step and ever so gently, Jesus again made His approach to me.

On the 9th of July 1986,[1] God said, "I God love you." My angel, immediately noticing my hesitation, asked me to keep these words saying that every word was given by God, and that God was near me. The next direct message from God was in July 1986.[1] The message was: "I have fed you, (spiritually), I came to give the food to you. Please help the others by giving them this food too. Flourish them, leading them to Me. I fed you, flourished you, fragranced you. Feed the others too. Help them and lead them to Me. I have given you Love, so follow Me. I have favoured you by giving you this food. Give it to the others too, to delight on it."

Then again, the 31st of July 1986,[1] this time Jesus came as the Sacred Heart and said to me: "In the middle of My Heart, have a place, My beloved. There you will live." On the 7th of August 1986,[1] the Father once more spoke to me giving me this message: "I God bind you with Me." Fearing, I asked Him very sharply because I was suspicious, that He name Himself. He answered, "Yahweh." I was filled with joy and love and already I had a burning in my soul from the yearning I had for Him. I said: "I love you Eternal Father." He

---

1. In the beginning, some messages were not written down, written on loose papers, or thrown away.

replied, "Love Me, praise Me, your God, I am your Eternal Father." I asked Him then: "Do you feel my happiness, my anguishes, my fears, my love, my confusions?" He replied, "Yes." Then I said: "In that case you know how I feel right now. You understand me fully," and He said with great tenderness: "Yes, I do, My beloved."

This again was my first communication for a long time after the rejection I had (out of fear). God went on, since He knew that I was wondering why He speaks to me. He said, "God loves you all, these messages are just a reminder, to remind you how your foundations began; deliver My message."

The very first messages I received were very short, as I explained in the beginning. They sounded more like telegrams than messages.

In the meantime, in spite of everything, I had not lost contact with the priests. But I had stopped talking about the messages to the one who had condemned them and had given me so much suffering. However, after some time, I decided to tell him that I was still receiving messages and writing them. So I showed him the notebooks instead of loose papers as before. I used any plain paper I could write on, but when the time came to start my mission, the Holy Spirit inspired me to open notebooks and number them.

I remember inviting the priest to my house so that I could tell him that I was still communicating with God. I thought I should inform him. I told him and he did not like it very much, but he asked me to show him the notebooks. I gave them to him to keep for a day. The next day I received a very harsh letter from him, telling me to burn all my notebooks and to go and tell all my friends who were reading them to forget everything. Somehow, I recognized Satan's harshness. I told my friends what he said, and they were very cross with him. I visited the priest and told him of their reaction. I took my notebooks away from him. He said that God is probably very angry with me now and that He abandoned me to my fate. He said that God was patient once or twice, but now, since I was not listening, He left me with the devil.

Already, the lessons of discernment from my angel were taking their effect and they became very useful to me in this particular moment. This time I could not be deceived. I answered the priest's letter and told him that his God is not my God. For his God is a cruel

God, quick to anger, impatient, intolerant and lacking love. His God forgives once or twice and then turns His back and throws the souls to hell if they do not listen, whereas the God I know of, the One who communicates with me daily, my God, is all love, infinitely patient, tolerant and tender. My God who speaks to me, and bends all the way from heaven, is meek, slow to anger, all merciful and envelops my soul with only love. My God who visits me every day in my room, the One whom he treats as the devil, surrounds my soul with peace and hope. My God nourishes me spiritually, augmenting my faith in Him. He teaches me spiritual things and reveals to me the Riches of His Heart.

After this he asked me to try once more for just a few days to stop writing to see what happened.

I allowed a few more days to pass without writing, as I had been asked by the priest. I prayed and asked again in my prayer, who was really guiding me in this special way? I had asked that if the messsages were really from Him, then I would like Him to tell me and hear Him say these words: "I Yahweh am guiding you." Nothing more. And this is what happened and God answered according to my prayer.

My communications continued and one day on December 15, 1986, (NB 1-6:34-35) God gave me this message: "Daughter, all Wisdom comes from Me. Do you want Wisdom?" Without realizing what God was offering me, I simply said "Yes" to Him. He then said that He would give me Wisdom but that I had to acquire Wisdom if I wanted Her. When He saw I was questioning myself on how to do this, He said that He is the Almighty and that He would teach me. I meditated on what God had offered me and the more I meditated the more I realized the tremendous Gift He was offering me. I realized too that I had not even thanked Him. So the following day I thanked Him and again He said that I would have to earn Wisdom, but He would help me and I should not get discouraged.

Do You Want To Serve Me?

The next thing I noticed was that Jesus was taking more and more the place of my angel. He came as the Sacred Heart. One day He surprised me by His question. He asked me if I wanted to serve Him, (for this mission). Fear overtook me and I hesitated. I did not allow this to be written like the rest of the other things. I was afraid that He might tell me to pack and leave my house to join a convent and become a nun. I was not ready and did not wish to do so either. My distrust disappointed Him, and His sadness did not escape me, since it was so obvious in the tone of His voice when He said these words, "I can abide in you in spite of your awesome weakness." I was very unhappy, because I had disappointed Him; on the other hand I was afraid of the unknown. These are the exact words:

> ..."were you to serve Me, I would reveal in you nothing but passion." I repeated, "passion," without understanding, and He said, "yes, passion. Will..." I lifted my hand not to write it, but I heard it all.

The whole night I spent time thinking of this; then I decided to plunge into the unknown and surrender to His Will. So I came back to Him with His question. I asked Him, "Do you want me to serve You?"

I immediately felt His joy and He said,

> "I do. I want it very much, Vassula. Come, I will show you how and where you can serve Me...work and serve Me as now, be as you are. I need servants who are able to serve Me where love is needed most. Work hard though, for where you are, you are among evil, unbelivers. You are in the vile depths of sin. You are going to serve your God where darkness prevails; you will have no rest. You will serve Me where every good is deformed into evil. Yes, serve Me among wretchedness, among wickedness and the iniquities of the world. Serve Me among Godless people, among those that mock Me, among those that pierce My Heart. Serve Me among My scourgers, among My condemners. Serve Me among those that recrucify Me and spit on Me. O Vassula, how I suffer! Come and console Me!...strive and suffer with Me, share My Cross..." (24th May 1987).

The teachings with God continued, and His communications were daily and to this day that I am writing, they are going on, for He said that His charism will stay with me up to my last day on earth.

Phase I

Dialogue with my angel Daniel   8. 5. 86

Be peaceful ♡ glory be to God for being good to have given you His Peace; I shall guard you from evil; be good and make a prayer now; Jesus will bring you closer to Him ♡ Dan

9. 5. 86

Peace ♡ I am near you; do not fear; forever I shall pray and guide you, I, forever shall guard you; be good; glory be to God; pray ♡ Dan

2

9 . 5 . 86

peace be upon you ; I shall guide you closer to God and make you a better person ; be good ; glory be to God ; may you go with the blessings of God your Heavenly Father ; amen, amen ♡

Daniel

10 . 5 . 86

peace to you ; I am your guardian angel ; I, forever shall guide you, forever guard you, Jesus purifies ; God loves you ; I am praying for you ;

praise Jesus ♡

3

I wonder if something wonderful will
happen.

maybe something wonderful happened
already ....

You mean that I changed?

yes; glory be to God for bringing you
close to Himself ♡ Dan

11 . 5 . 86

peace ♡

Are you happy that I am closer to God
now ?

yes ♡

Is it enough ?

4

no ♡ you must make further progress;
I will help you ♡ Daniel ♡

12. 5. 86

peace unto you; pray ♡ I want to
detach you and bond you to God;
wait and you shall see; you will give
me great joy .... need God; Jesus purifies
you, go to Him, meet Him through
prayer ♡

Later on:

listen to me; love God more because

5

He loves you and is near you now and forever; make a further effort, my beloved; read in the Bible: Daniel; concentrate especially in prayer; God blesses you ♡ Daniel

Later on again:

glory be to God for giving you to me to guide you nearer to Him ♡ now you do a prayer; do not fear me; have faith in God on whom you should lean, peacefully; He loves you; glorify Him, praise Him;

6

glory be to God; praise the Lord ♡

$$Daniel$$

13. 5. 86

peace unto you;

$$Yahweh$$

loves you; I must bond you to
Him more; love

$$Yahweh$$

more ♡ Daniel

14. 5. 86

$$Yahweh$$

7

loves you; Yahweh

gives you light,

Yahweh

gives you sight and eternal life; need

Yahweh

our God Almighty ♡ Dan

Later on:

I will fight any evil spirit that attempts
to approach you, by praying ♡ Dan

15. 5. 86

Yahweh

8

will guide you ♡ be good with all
people and with everything; this way of
writing is a gift from God;
praise the Lord ♡   Glory be to God ♡
Dan

17. 5. 86

Jesus forgives sins and purifies; I am
coming to you with peace in His Name;
pray; I am praying for you ♡

Later on:

peace; peace; love all the things that
God has given you; may your love

9

grow constantly and may it increase ♡
Daniel

18 . 5 . 86

peace be with you; come to Jesus and
love Him; glory be to God! .... glorify
God; come to Jesus, He died for you;
need Him; I shall guide you to approach
Jesus; come and yearn to learn the
Good things ♡ Dan

19. 5. 86

I will help you and teach you to
discern ♡ I will teach you to

10

recognize who is with you*; Jesus loves you eternally: " fear not, for I am here and I love you all; "

(This was Jesus speaking. My angel quoted Him.)

20.5.86

praise the Lord for He is good; glorify Him for He is near; Jesus brings Peace and Love to all; be good, be good ♡   Dan

* While writing: to discern an evil spirit from God or my angel.

11

21. 5. 86

glory be to God; I will pray for you;
I will teach you God's Law; I talk
now for God; God

Yahweh

selected you to be His pupil and teach
you all about Himself and His Son
Jesus Christ; praise the Lord; go in
peace ♡ Daniel

23. 5. 86

peace be upon you; I will bond you
more to God, those bonds will strengthen

12

your soul giving peace to your soul ♡
lean on God ; I love you ; love ♡ God ;
I will tidy a place for you ; I will
wait for you, I will take you to God ....
collect money and give it to the poor
needy souls ; give them better clothes* ; be
generous ; glory be to God ♡   Daniel
♡

* All that I earned in my exhibition was
given to the poor. I bought stacks of the local
outfit, saris for women and lungis for men
distributing them to Christians and Moslems alike
—   Later on just before Xmas I went with two
friends from house to house begging for donation
for the poor. I lost a few friends for this act.

13

24.5.86

Jesus died for you;

" fear not for I am near you;"

(I immediately got alarmed.)

Who said this?

God said it; I shall clothe you in a white gown and I will make you pure* in Jesus' Presence; praise the Lord ♡ Daniel

* He was allowed by God to give me a special purification, later on, allowing me to see my sins with God's Eyes.

14

25. 5. 86

Vassula, nothing lasts where you are, but where I live, all lasts forever, forever; Glory be to God for bringing you closer to Himself ♡

Yahweh loves you; live in peace; lean on

Yahweh

for

Yahweh

restores; give glory to Him;

" Peace to all, Peace to all beings on earth; "

* This last line was from God.

15

Phase II　　　　　　　　　　　　　　26.5.86

be everything that God likes; turn to faith;
be holy; reach to God and come with a
clean soul before Him;

Yahweh

loves you; go and pray; glorify God
and praise Him ♡　Dan

27. 5. 86

peace be with you; I will do all that
God wants me to do; I will lead you
to God ♡　Dan

16

28. 5. 86

Father! Father of the Heavens, lead everything and give me strength!

What are you saying?

I was praying to the Father in Heaven;
Glory be to God; Jesus is always with
you; call Jesus in your prayers; I will
lead you to your Father;

(I started to fear that I was being deceived.)

fear not, my messages do no harm to
you; love God, love Him more ♡

Daniel

17

30 . 5 . 86

peace be with you ; lead a pure life,
I shall pray for you ; love Jesus Christ,
He loves you ♡

" fear not, for I am near ; come to Me,
I am here ";*

(I asked my angel,)

Where are you usually ?

I am where you are ;

Could you see me as clear as I see things ?

yes ;

* I ignored this sentence that came from Jesus
out of fear I was deceived. I spoke to my angel
then and pretended I never heard anything.

18

Where are you when I run down the stairs?

I am with you;

Where are you now?

I am near you;

Where will you be when I die?

you will meet me; I shall be by your

side;

Tell me something ....

I love God;   glorify God 🜚 Dan

31. 5. 86

peace; peace be with you; God loves

you showing His love; God loves you

19

all, far beyond anybody's understanding;
love 'God', for God is good; love Him
with all your strength ♡   Daniel

1. 6. 86

peace to you; be good; stop reading
those books *, the Bible preaches the
Truth ♡ Dan

2. 6. 86

peace, peace to you; remember God;
He did wonders from the beginning;

* Bad litterature

20

all Glory comes from God; God will
bond you to Him; go with the grace
of our Lord Jesus Christ; every one ends,
from end comes beginning; leave in
peace ♡ Dan

6. 6. 86

(I recalled a dream I had a few months back.)
I dreamt (vision) that you protected me
from a snake.

how could I leave you when that snake
was savouring you! go in the grace of
our Lord Jesus Christ ♡ Dan

This is what I saw:

21

I was sitting on a sofa in my house.
Opposite me on another sofa sat all my
family. — Suddenly I heard a slight noise on
my left side at the corner of that room, which
was rather obscure; and from that dark corner
I saw crawling on the floor a snake. That snake
was my pet; It came out of its corner to search
for food since I had stopped feeding it. It found
a dish with 3 grapes, which it swallowed in its
hunger entirely but it was not sufficient and it
creeped in the kitchen to look for more, while passing between the sofas. I immediately pulled my
feet up, fearing now since I had become its
enemy and fearing it senses this, it would strike
me. I feared very much. So I got up to catch
it, lest it would strike one of my family. The
minute the snake realized my intentions it prepared itself to strike me. I feared so much that
I grasped the top of a cupboard and hanging
from there I coiled up my legs; and while
the snake stood up on its rear I heard a
voice. Upon hearing this voice the snake feared,
and went away from me. I sprung (cont.)

21a

cont.

down and ran to see who was this.
I saw a tall man, and I understood that
he was my guardian angel. He said:
" Why do you fear? " I said: " I'm
afraid from the snake, it is loose." He
said: " I will go and chase it away.
He went in the kitchen and when I was
going away I thought: " Perhaps I should
also help him." So I went also in the
kitchen. This man opened wide open
the kitchen door, then took a stick and
with that tried to cast it out, while I
was making so much noise, waving my
hands and stamping my feet to frighten
it away. Every time the snake wanted to
escape and was coming my way, I stood,
stamping my feet, blocking its way. It
panicked and in its panick it went out
of the house. Once out, the guardian angel
slammed the door shut. There was
a window on the right side of the door.
Both my angel and I looked out to
see what will happen to the snake.

21 b

It went out sliding down the stairway. But the stairway was very busy with people going up and down and so, frightened lest it would be tread upon it made its way back to the house. But it found the door shut. Then, it really panicked. It slipped down the stairway very quickly into a hall and out of the wide glass-doors of the hall. The minute it crossed the threshold of that glass-door the snake was transformed into a gigantic ugly toad. It find itself surrounded by snow and icy weather. There were people who saw it out there and the minute they raised the alarm, from a toad it took the form and shape of a woman. But the evil spirit was recognized and the people caught it and strapped it tying it. — While doing this I felt that the straps were not so secure and that one day again it will escape.

22

7. 6. 86

peace to you; start praying; I want
you to "progress spiritually"; Peace is
God; remember God's Word; Dan

8. 6. 86

I will heal you spiritually ♡ Dan

9. 6. 86

I will defend you; I will guard you
and give you every protection; you
need, never fear ♡

Later on:

glory be to God; never fear death;

23

the end*¹ becomes wonderful; praise Dad;*²
Daniel

10. 6. 86

peace be with you; I prayed for you to
end your discussions that will never
progress you, nor will you earn anything
from them; turn to God and lean
on Him; glory be to God ♡ Dan

12. 6. 86

come and pray; the end of your life
is the beginning only of eternity;

*¹ After death.
*² He called our Eternal Father: Dad = Abba

24

love God deeply; give God everything;
lead a pure life; worship God;
forgive; every meaning of your life should
sum up to good ♡   Dan

13. 6.86

peace be with you; be good; worship
God everywhere you go; worship God
for He is good; praise the Messiah;
you will work for God; every way of
worshipping God is good; leave now
with peace ♡   Daniel

25

14 . 6 . 86

peace be with you; need Jesus to give you
more faith; this gift* was given from
God; make a prayer ♡ Dan

17 . 6 . 86

peace be with you; learn good Emmanuel's
Word; read every day the Bible and
your soul shall progress; lead a meek life ♡
Dan

18 . 6 . 86

peace be with you; these messages are a

---

* To hear and to write : these messages.

26

means of meditation; reading the Bible
progresses your soul; feel loved;

Yahweh
is Love; feel His Love;

Yahweh
loves you ♡ Daniel

19 . 6 . 86

peace ♡ peace be with you; Vassula, be
good in every way; lean on God and
love Him; praise Jesus ♡ Dan

20 . 6 . 86

peace be with you; " I Jesus love you;

27

(Direct words from our Lord.)

22. 6. 86

peace be with you ; turn to Faith and keep
it forever ; Faith helps you ; Faith in God
gives you love ; Faith brings you closer to
the Most High ; Faith gives you Peace and
Love ; praise the Lord Jesus ; God is a
loving God ; pray, feel loved by Jesus ;
everybody is loved by God ; praise God ;
glorify God ; every man is loved by God ;
glory be to God for restoring you ♡

Dan

28

23. 6. 86

God is Peace ♡ Peace is Love ♡ Dan

24. 6. 86

years shall flow by but Jesus will remain
God's Beloved Son ♡

Phase III

24. 6. 86

peace be with you; years shall flow by
and Jesus will still be healing; Jesus
has done healings that revealed His Glory;
Jesus loves all of you; remember what
He said: "I love you all; I have
given you forever Myself"; Jesus died to

29

save you all; Jesus conquered Death and
is glorified ♡ Dan

25. 6. 86

peace be with you; purifying you further
will progress you; take the Road that
leads to God; I will be praying for
your perfection; love Jesus; turn to God ♡
Daniel

26. 6. 86

peace be with you; who was near you
from the beginning of your life?

My mother (of course) doctors etc.

30

I was there too*; I will always be with you; go eagerly to pray ♡ Daniel

27. 6. 86

peace be with you ♡ who is your Father?

(I was surprised by his question.)

God is my Father.

praise Him; love Him and glorify Him ♡

1. 7. 86

(I went to Switzerland to visit my mother.)

be good with the widow ♡ (On purpose he called her 'widow' to teach me that our Blessed Mother _is_ the only Mother we have.)

* My angel wanted to tell me that he was there _from_ the beginning.

31

2. 7. 86

pray; be good; glory be to God ♡ have
the blessings from the Heavenly Father
and His Son Jesus Christ ♡ Dan

♡

8. 7. 86

(I was afraid that all these writings were
   not good.)

peace be with you ♡ feel how you have
been healed from your guilt;
Vassula, how?

By these messages.

yes; how then can these meditations be
bad? thank and praise the Lord for

32

healing you .... have you heard of
flowers that healed ?

Yes.

I, your angel formed* you through God;
I flourished you, I fragranced you; I
have healed you through God; Jesus
blessed you ♡ praise Jesus; I have done
all the things that God wanted me to
do ♡ " fear not for I am with you
always ; rely on the Bible; tell them
that I heal the sick ; fear not, I will

* *That is: " taught me."*

33

heal you ; flowers do heal .... (Jesus
was speaking, then my angel came back
to say :)

Jesus is your Healer ; you delight Him ;
Jesus left you blooming ♡ Dan

8 . 7 . 86

pray and love

Yahweh ;
praise Jesus and rely on the Bible,
meditate ♡ Dan

9 . 7 . 86

peace be with you ♡ (I was doubting again.)

34

have you loved Yahweh
always?

No, only after the writings.

have you had peace since the beginning
of your love for Yahweh?

...* answer!

I am happy.

never have two loves;

I have only one.

* I kept silent for a while, trying to figure
out what my angel meant by 'peace'.

35

flourish then others ♡   Daniel God's
servant ♡

12. 7. 87

peace be with you; follow Jesus; glorify
God; I mean it; go in peace ♡
Dan

13. 7. 87

peace be with you; Jesus has forgiven
you;

Will one day religion fade out?
never!

I do not have much time these days to
write.

36

I understand; feel peaceful; have Jesus as your Peace; you will meet aged author* ♡ Dan

14. 7. 86

peace be with you; aged author shall guide you* ♡

    Will I meet an author?

all in good time; Jesus guides all of you, dear; never fear; I shall protect you; go in peace ♡ Dan

* I met this "aged author", not before 1991: The "aged author" my angel was talking about happens to be Fr. Michael O'Carroll, my spiritual counsellor, author of several encyclopedias, books and articles, and my guide.

37

16. 7. 86

O God! have her follow You *....

Daniel were you asking this for me?

yes; peace be with you ♡ lead a good
life; have God's blessings; I love you;
love Jesus ♡   Dan

17. 7. 86

peace be with you; glory be to God ♡

18. 7. 86

(In this day I was tired, edgy and agressive.)

peace be with you; have peace .... peace,

* This prayer came from my angel and sounded
more of a lament than a supplication.

38

peace ... peace ... peace ... peace be with you ♡ peace be with you ; have peace;

(But I went on complaining and complaining, and he was listening patiently.)

I know .... have peace .... you are tired; .... I prayed for you .... have you read the Gospels to have peace? I have prayed for you to take the Hand of Jesus ; do you feel better?

Yes.

meditate more ♡ peace be with you .... rest my beloved; have your rest ....

39

I have now made you feel glad*;
peace be with you ♡   Dan

20. 7. 86

rely on the Bible; pray; name Jesus in
your prayers; need Jesus;

Do you realize that I do not quite
realize all this?

yes, but you will one day; rely on
Jesus ♡   Daniel

22. 7. 86

peace be with you ♡ ponder on what

* My angel did in fact.

40

Jesus wants;

To love God, but truly love Him. To
follow His commandments, to worship
Him and to be good.

yes; deliver yourself to Jesus; pray
more; meditate more; you have to ....
praise Jesus who helped you ♡

Do I have any proof of all this?

you are the proof; Jesus flourished you;

The priest said that this is not a way
God works.

how did you love God?

Through the messages!

41

so feel peaceful, God guided you to Him;
Love God till the end; pray; glorify God;
Dan.

25 . 7 . 86

peace be with you; need only God; love
Yahweh;
love Him more;   Yahweh
loves you more than you can imagine ♡
give this message to others to; lean on
God; go in peace, dear, and pray ♡ Dan;

29 . 7 . 86

(Doubts again?)
peace be with you; how did you lead

42

your cousin to read your Bible? what are
the reasons that makes you do all this?

I want everybody to feel like me, happy, for
loving God. I also learned many things through
the writings.

God loves you far more than you are able
to understand; praise God ♡ Dan

29. 7. 86

peace be with you ♡

I sometimes think my appearance is not right
for this gift, so it bothers me.

your appearance has no harm; give no
heed to your appearance; Jesus told His

43

disciples that clean hearts are healthier than
what appears to be good from outside, but
from within is corrupt ♡ Jesus healed you
from your guilt; He healed you from
leading a false life; I desired so much
that Jesus would heal you ♡ Glory be to
God! have my blessings; pray, love God,
He loves you; He will help you; have

Yahweh

for your peace ♡   Daniel

(Fears and ♡ doubts again.) 31. 7. 86
peace be with you; glory be to God;

44

do you feel peaceful?

Yes.

so how could this be from Satan if you feel peaceful? you have learned to love God more than you ever did; then, you want others as well to love God, glorifying God, this is against Satan! would Satan work and try to destroy himself? I will guide you and bond you more to God;

every time you doubt think what you have earned from these texts ♡

(Later :)

45

How do you feel Daniel?

I love

Yahweh

with all my strength, with all my might;
I work for

Yahweh

and always will ♡ Daniel, God's servant

5. 8. 86

peace be with you;

Why was I given this gift?

God wished it; Jesus has helped you
find the Light;

If they say, 'why did He give the Light

46

to you and not to us ?'

Jesus gives the Light to all of you;

They might say, 'who do you think you
are'? You are not even a nun.'

you are God's servant; God has given
you this gift to bring you to Him and
lead others too to Him; He loves you
and wants you all near Him; He
means to bring you all back to Him;
Glory be to God;

Daniel

47

6. 8. 86

peace be with you ♡ praise the
Most High God, Yahweh;

I am afraid to show the messages. I love
God deeply, but I am afraid to show
the messages. Day and night I am
thinking only of this.

God will give you His Peace and His
Strength when the time comes, to show
the messages; God will want you to
give those messages to everyone; pray;
feel loved, God will help you;

Dan

48

7. 8. 86

peace be with you; you are to deliver Dominus' message;

Maybe all this is not true, maybe it is a joke!

what makes you think it is a joke?

Because this _is_ unusual, is it not?

yes;

You admit then that this is not very common either.

it is not very common .... did you believe before this in God?

I did. But I did not love Him. I had no feelings for Him.

49

God feels everything;

.... Can we talk?

yes;

Why has all this started?

God wished that you love Him;

This is not common, I mean this sort of communication. You agree, don't you?

*

yes ♡

why do you draw a heart?
(I said it agressively because I was somewhat afraid of this phenomena).

*I felt my angel amused but at the same time full of love as parents are with their babe's when they do funny things.

So

you delight me ;

You know that you scare me sometimes ?

yes ; you need not fear ; you will be working for Jesus Christ ; you will be helping others to grow spiritually ;

* I God bind you to Me ;

(I feared) give me your name !

Yahweh

But I can't understand, we have already the Bible, so why do we need messages ?

(My angel replied.) so you do feel that

* God intervened

51

all has been given in the Bible?

yes. That is why I do not see the reason of all this. I mean nothing is new.

God wants these messages to be given;

Is there a special reason why me?

no; God loves you all; these messages are just a reminder, to remind you how your foundations begun; deliver my message;

Daniel, <u>who</u> are you?

God's servant;

Daniel

52

7. 8. 86

peace be with you; praise Yahweh; God does wonders. believe .... feel happy that Jesus Christ healed you*; pray more and think what all this is about; realize the importance; realize that the given messages are from

Heaven

from Hall of God,

Yahweh,

wrote,

* spiritually

S 3

Dominus Seigneur,
have you realized that these pages are
given by God?

God preached to you!

Himself?

Yes! write peacefully; I have done all
that God wanted me to do; glorify
Yahweh and follow Jesus; God has
found a way to teach you; praise Him;
this is God's Gift; God has
helped you and always will; Dan

54

Phase IV

31. 8. 86

peace be with you; I bless you; I have
wept on you, lamented on you when I
was reminded about your past;

Who reminded you?

God; He gave me a vision of your
past *¹ and when you were unhappy;
I wept also when I had to tell
you to go *²; I wept; God wanted it this
way; I will go now to a reunion

---

*¹ Before my conversion.
*² God had given him an order to go in time
God left me in the desert, for purification.
    (Read details :

55

of saints ;

Do you have a meeting ?

yes; we pray ; the Holy Spirit will guide you soon; I have worked with you to flourish you; have peace; you will progress ; Jesus will soon call you;

Vassula, you can call Jesus anytime;

Can I ?

yes, He will work with you ; Glory be to God ; read the Holy Bible to acquire knowledge ;

Daniel

56

24. 8. 86

peace be with you; live in peace and joy; I will give you Peace; I will augment your joy; I will work with you; welcome Me with love;

I am your Peace;

Who are you who say I, and I and I? *

I am Jesus Christ ♡

5. 9. 86

full you shall be many;

* I asked rather impertinently thinking it was my guardian angel. I thought he was over-doing it because the tone of his voice suddenly had taken such authority and superiority, like God's.

57

Please explain to me what you mean.

when you will be filled with My Holy
Spirit you will be able to guide others
to Me and you shall multiply; it
means to receive My Holy Spirit in you;

6. 9. 86

peace be with you; love My Mother; She
loves you; love Her;*

I feel so nice and free!

you are far more free than ever before;

* Jesus was speaking to me.

58

Can I ask You one thing?

yes;

And You will NEVER forget it?

no;

I would like to augment my faith and my love for You and if You see me slip or stumble, restore me again. I ask this from You, Jesus Christ.

I will help you; sleep not, for the dawn is near; every time you feel weak, pray and call Me, I will be near you My beloved;

Did You my Lord say: " In the middle of My Heart have a place, there you

59

shall live?"

yes; I will make a place for you; are
you willing to live in Me?

Give me your full name again. (I was
suspicious and careful.)

Jesus Christ, Beloved Son of God;

Am I accepted?

you are welcomed in My Heart; I will
teach you to work so that you meet
Me;

(My angel now speaks)

here is today's message: read the Bible more;

60

Should I read all the day?

no; Jesus does not work in this way;
He does not wish you to have endless
hours of work; Jesus wishes that learning
becomes a happiness; He wants you to
love it ♡

Dan

7.9.86

peace be with you; come and repent;

How do I do it?

pray and say:

"Father, forgive me for all my sins;"

61

when you will make this prayer, praise
God with all your heart, feeling your
words;

Daniel

Λ God love you;

Please give me your name.

Yahweh; never feel miserable because Λ
will reach for you and Λ will lift you
to Me; always remember this; Λ love
you and Λ will protect you from evil.
remember, Λ will call you more, when
you hear My calls, know it is Λ, Yahweh

62

who called you; I will meet you in this way; I have given you this gift and I will always be near you; pray more;

(Later on :)

I am here, I am here;

Who is it? (I had doubts to believe it was Jesus and I wanted to dismiss Him remembering what the priest had told me, that God does not speak that way.)

Jesus Christ;

Is it you Daniel? (I tried to ignore Him and was looking for my Angel).

no;

Daniel?

63

no; no, it is I, Jesus, remember what I told you before, to turn to Me; lean on Me;

Who is with me? (I feared and had doubts).

it is I, Jesus;

(Accepting this, I wept.)

why do you weep? I love you;

(I wept because I remembered His sufferings).

dying was to deliver you! I have delivered you; have peace; call Me and I will be with you;

64

If anybody from the street saw this, they would laugh on me.

why? for worshipping Me?

For instance, if I showed this to other priests than fr. Karl they would mock me, disbelieve me; they'll say I am mad; they'll say it's Satan or my subconscious mind!

how will they feel if I had worked with them in this way?

I don't really Know; some would be convinced. If it was a bishop, they would say they are divine, but also some would think he's lost his mind because of too much religion going in his head.

have you thought before of God?

No.

do you feel you have changed?

Yes, a lot!

why?... why?

If I may put it right: because God called me and preached to me.

yes; blessed are the pure in heart for they shall <u>see</u> God;

(Suddenly all hell broke loose. The beast asked me to worship him. I told him: "go!" He left. He had said that if I would worship him instead, he will glorify me. I told him to disappear. So he did.)

9. 9. 86

I, Yahweh, love you; realize that I have

2

been with you;

In prayer?

in this way too; I bless you .... why,
why have you been refusing Me? I am
Yahweh; fear not! fear not! .... have
you felt happy?*

yes.

how then would this be, if it was from
the evil one?

Give me your name! (I was suspicious).

* During the encounters and the dictations.

3

Yahweh is My Name; love Me; I Yahweh
will help you;

10. 9. 86

peace be with you; I am Yahweh; I
am teaching you and reminding you who
founded you and who loved you; I
want your intimacy; I love you;
feel loved; I will protect you; I will
console you;

(I suddenly thought that God cannot speak
just like that to me, a nobody, so I
thought that probably I am mistaken and
that I misunderstood. It was probably my
angel).

4

Daniel?

why do think it is Daniel?

Because I was approached by Daniel in the
beginning. — Daniel?

no;

Daniel?

no;

DANIEL?

no; I am Yahweh; are you ready to
hear Me?

I bless You, Father, You who taught me.
I am happy now.

why?

5

Because You helped me.

I finally brought you near Me ;

May I ask Your name again?

Yahweh ;

Please understand why I double - check.

I do ; are you ready to hear Me ?

Yes !

are you happy to receive Me every time ?

Yes. I am overwhelmed with joy.

why ?

Because I am filled up with love from You,
my God, which pours out of me like a fountain;
and it is You, God, who taught me and

6

helped me in this.

help the others too to feel the same way;

How?

I, Yahweh, shall guide you;

12. 9. 86

peace be with you; anytime you want, meet Me; every time you feel upset,* know that it is not I who wrote it; any message that worries you, I, Yahweh have not written it. every time you feel unhappy know it is not from Me; feel free and

* Upset: about a message.

7

meet Me; I, Yahweh am Peace; welcome
Me in your prayers; read My Word;

I am asking myself sometimes why all this?
because I want to remind you how much
love I have for all of you; read with
love My Word;

My Father in Heaven have you <u>really</u> called me?

beloved, I have;

17. 9. 86

peace be with you; it is I, Yahweh; I
will help you understand My Word and
I will teach you; augment your love

8

for Me;

I do not want to do anything wrong that would destroy all this. I'll be very sad.

I will not wait for this; I will comfort you; I am your Eternal Father who loves you, who created you; I have, when you first breathed, held you close to Me; love one another because you are all created by My Hands; all of you are My children; remember who founded you? do not venture elsewhere; come to Me and I will cover you with My blessings;

9

I will pour all My love on you; <u>love</u>
<u>Me more</u>; the Path to Me is among you,
take it and it will lead you to Me;
with arms opened I shall welcome you;
I shall embrace you and bless you; pray
for righteousness;

19. 9. 86

peace be with you; I am Peace; do not
rebel against Me; all those who have
ears listen; listen to My calls; why, why
have you forsaken Me? I, who love you
so much; why are you so few who

10

remember Me? have I God, not founded you? have I not loved you, cherished you and blessed you? are you diverted by fantasies? is this what you claim to be? have you not felt me? purify yourselves for I am within you; are you, beloved, like leaves, when autumn comes, you shrivel and fall? children, children, come back to Me; fill up My Holy Places and delight Me;

Dear Father in Heaven, what if they will not listen?

11

every man has ears, they should know why I made them for; I have given them eyes to distinguish between darkness and light; augment My happiness, daughter, by keeping your love for Me; welcome Me in your prayers; I am your Heavenly Father, God Almighty; read My Word; rely on it ♡

21. 9. 86.

(Doubts again that God can speak to me. This time Jesus spoke).

Glory be to God;

12

Is that you Daniel?

why, <u>why</u> Daniel?

Daniel is the one who always glorifies God.

are you quite sure that only Daniel glorified God?

(Here I understood; I smiled.)

why are you doubting? I am Jesus Christ, God's Beloved Son; — I love you all;

23. 9. 86

peace be with you; hear Me; I God will never never abandon you; live in peace; do not feel worried Vassula;

13

look at yourself, you are the proof of
My Love; I have converted you; you are
radiating My Love; I, God, preached to
you, I held you close to Me because you
are My Own; feel how much I love
you;

Can I ask You why You have given
me this Gift?

I gave you this blessing, accept it; call
Me <u>any time</u> you wish; I, God, will
call you irrespective of who you are; —
blessed are the little ones for they shall

14

inherit the kingdom of God;
blessed are the pure in heart, for they
shall see God; — Vasula, read
this over and over again and understand
it; believe Me, anyone who has got
both, the barriers will be shattered and
they shall enter in God's Hall; Abba
will welcome them ♡

4. 10. 86

peace be with you; come, come to Me
delight Me; are you going to ask Me
your question?

15

Do You feel we are ignoring You?

yes; so beware of sleep... Heaven's morning star is soon to be seen; would not I, who am Your Father and care for you not warn you? I am Yahweh, your Creator and you are all My children; – where, where do you think you will go? did you ever give it a thought? did you really believe you just came on your own? had you believed that I had left you? or that I never existed? did you really believe that My Word was all a dialect

16

of collected Hebrew fairy tales? hear Me,
My Word is alive and the Truth; it
is to enlighten you and to help you understand who I am, what you are; My
Word is to help you find Me; children,
children, is your religion based on scientific
understanding? do not push Me away
and go on hiding from Me; how
did you leave yourselves drift away from
Me? <u>believe in the Resurrection;</u>
believe how your soul will go on living;
do not drift away and live a life

17

analysing how you came to be, since I
tell you that you all come from Me; I
God am your Creator; I have created
you because I love life; I made you to
live in My Light; I created the heavens,
I created everything; how else did you
think all this was done? the heavens
were not just there, and you did not
just happen to be there; — creation,
is done by Me; let your academies teach
you more of how you came to be; let
them find the answer to the vital question:

18

' why do you exist? some of you do not even bother to ask any questions accepting life as it comes, not believing that your soul keeps on living once you die; blind! blind! and deaf! refusing to see and hear, are you afraid of finding the Truth? I am the Truth; are you fearing to find Me? have you closed your eyes so that you deny Me? is it simpler for you that way, or are you searching? I am the Way ♡ I am the Way and I love you; ♡ I am the Light that

19

shines for everyone to see <u>the Truth</u>;
beloved children, My Heart pains to see
you all sleeping; how could I not
come to you and warn you? how
could I leave you when evil is prowling
among you like a wolf waiting to
devour you? I want to wake you up
so that you meet Me; I am longing to
see this glorious moment ... will your
sleep last forever*? — I, God, have called
you; I, God, still call you; come
to Me

♡ * God seemed to be talking to Himself,
just here.

20

- Later that afternoon -
(I have problems again to assimilate that
it is really God speaking to me.)

peace be with you. remember Who
founded the world and the heavens?
Who created you? Who blessed you
and loved you? Who gave His only
begotten Son to the world to save the
world? *

Many would not believe that this is from
You, they will say:"it is not from God.
God does not work in this way."
how does God work? does God do any
wonders?

* Jesus was speaking of His Father

21

Yes, He always did. But it's me. I am the problem.

are you wicked? are you worshipping another god?

I do not worship another god.

are you calling other gods in your prayers?

No. (Then I felt our Blessed Mother's presence near me.)

love Her; remember when I was on the Cross? what were the words I said? I said that She is your Mother too; She loves you and cares for you; Abba gives to whom He pleases; accept

22

what God is giving you;

How did You feel when the priest was telling me that You would have thrown me out of the Church, and if I knocked at the door of the Church You would not have opened because You can refuse.

I wept; I buried My Face in My Hands and wept; My Church is for every man; I welcome anyone who knocks at My door;* I, Jesus, will open the door; I am your Redeemer who loves you ♡

* Mt 7 : 7. "Knock and the door <u>will</u> be opened to you."

23

5. 10. 86

peace be with you; I brought you up so
that you may be My bearer;

When will I know to whom I should give
the messages?

leave these things to Me; I will name

you, Vassula: My bearer;

I do so many mistakes.

I accept your mistakes because you are only
learning now; I am Peace; I will never
leave you with a message that brings
you unrest; I will give you My messages

* God started to teach me to discern.

24

then, when the time is right, I will guide you to deliver them; are you willing to do this for Me?

Name Yourself before I accept.

I am Yahweh, your God;

I accept to be guided by Yahweh.

any message that will give you anxiety or any message that will leave you worried, does not come from Me; I am Peace and Love; I want you to feel peaceful working with Me;

25

9. 10. 86

peace be with you, I God want My children to come to Me; I want My children to live in peace;

Were You troubled when You wrote down the message of the eighth?

beloved, how can I not be? when they are living in a period of blood; My messages cry out for Peace! I, God, am the Almighty and I am able to discipline destruction and withdraw evil, guarding peace and order, but I want My children to wake up; with all My children

26

back, I, God, will be full of happiness;
I am full of Love, full of Pity, I am
your Consoler ♡

11. 10. 86

peace be with you;

Why is it me who receives God's messages?

I, God, choose; I have chosen you; I
brought you up so that I give you My
messages;

Did You decide it recently?

here is My answer: before you were
formed in your mother's womb, I, God,

27

planned it; learn how I work ♡

I made so many sins in the meantime!
every sin is forgiven by Me when you
ask to be forgiven; be near Me now
and I shall guide you; I am still teaching
you, so do not get discouraged when you
do errors; I, God, am the Almighty;
I have the whole universe in the palm
of My Hand;

Lord, no one will believe all this ....
The sceptics will say I am mad or
others, my subconcious.

leave those to Me; I am Yahweh your

28

Creator; I am leading you, Vassula, you need not fear; remember, I led many others before you; I overthrew kings and kingdoms, I straightened paths so that My Word would be known; I am the same*; hear Me, I helped all those that followed Me; I will always help whoever follows Me; remember, I am always with you;

---

* By this I understood that NO ONE will be able to STOP Him and His message.

29

12. 10. 86

peace be with you; <u>any word you feel</u>
<u>is not right and troubles you, feel free</u>
<u>to correct it</u>, I, God give you that
feeling ♡ Vassula, are you happy?

More than happy, overwhelmed. (I can't
describe it when I feel God's Love on me.)

(Later on my angel came.)

I am Dan; I am before you ♡

Dan! how come?

remember what I taught you? be careful to recognize and discern; work in
this way and you will progress; glory

30

be to God ;

Why did you come ?

because I love you very much ; lean on
Yahweh for He is your Redeemer ;

Why did you come ?

I asked to come ; remember, lean on
God ; I love you, I mean it ; lean
on Yahweh and go in peace ; *

I Dan bless you, in the Name of

---

* The day before this message, I confessed to
God that I loved my angel Daniel and felt
comfortable with him and peaceful, but God
asked me to leave now Daniel and be with Him
because He Himself wanted to teach me. And I
had been sad thinking I'll never speak to Dan again

31

God the Father, His Beloved Son Jesus Christ and the Holy Spirit; I am God's servant;

Do you remember how I was eight months back?

I remember, you were indifferent to God;

Yes. Do you remember when God's Name was mentioned and written by you?

yes;

You said: " God is near and loves you." It was like you were telling me:" today the weather is fine. " That's how my attitude was.

worse ....

32

Then all the attacks I've had. I felt like
I went through a PURGATORY.

accept it that way;

I imagine that maybe it's like this that
one goes through after he dies. PURGATORY,
then, when one is purified, everything is
clearer. One is more pure and elevated.
..... I love God <u>so</u> much! ..... Does God
really want us to be intimate with Him?

yes; call Him, turn to God;

Can I?

yes; the Light is here ...* I love you,
I will help you, I am Peace;

* (My angel gave way to Jesus' Presence.
Jesus took over.)

33

feel Me*; I will shelter you, I will protect you ♡

God asked me to write down His Message He had given us on the 8.10.86.

yes! peace be with you; I God am calling you now; here is My Message: remember, I God live, I live, I exist; are you still doubting? are you still analising how? are you spending your whole lifetime analising Me, diagnosing Me, having endless discussions

* Jesus wanted me to feel His Presence.

34

whether I Am or not? why? hear
Me: when I first founded the earth I was
filled up with joy; I spread out the stars
and named each one of them; later on,
with love and happiness I created you,
with My own Hands I formed you giving
you the breath of life; I raised you
and blessed you; – I am your Holy
Father; then I sent you wise
men to guide you and teach you how
all Creation began; I revealed Myself
to you* to teach you how your

* To people like me, who forgot God.

35

foundations begun, who your Creator is;
I, God am your Father; and now,
you spend generation after generation sifting
Me, analising Me, dwelling in perpetual
darkness, fleeing from Me, creating chaos
among you; can you not understand
how you slaughter each other, creating
wars, hating each other, eradicating
races and towns, leaving your homeland desolate, widowing your women, making orphans of your children, manifesting
only hatred? where? where have

36

all My blessings gone? where is the love
I blessed you with gone? where are My
children, where are they, where have they
gone? I cannot recognize them anymore*,
where have they gone? Evil has called
them hiring them as weapons to blow out
all light left in them and destroy them
completely; <u>I pain and weep</u> to see My
beloved children lost forever! am I
radiating anger, hate or destruction?

* Filled with grief, God said these words. For God
created man in the image of Himself and this image
now was destroyed by man himself.

37

did you ever believe I am a God of war? am I not a God of Peace and Love? hear Me, O children, created by My Own Hands, coming from the crib I made for you, coming from My Hands which held you close to My Breast, blessed from the core of My Heart, healed by My Beloved Son, Jesus Christ, loved and cherished by Me, what have you become? where do you think you are going? hear Me: return to Me, come back to Me, I, who love you; learn from Me, I am Holy,

38

be Holy, live Holy; do not deny Me
telling Me you do not know Me and
that you never knew Me! have you ima-
gined that I never existed and that My
Word was only to entertain Hebrews?
believe in My Word for I am its Author;

My Word is alive as I am alive,
was it not, you could not have been;
hear Me, life is but a brief passage and
you are but briefly going through it, with
an eclipsed life how could you feel
happy? how could any one of you

39

believe you are able to survive in darkness? not one reed lives without light; I am the light and being in Me you will live; I shine for everyone to see and be in My light; My Heart pains to see you in the evil's claws, remaining in darkness; I can hear you all, how you are doubting and how you are analising Me, how you turn your faces away from Me, refusing to hear, refusing to see! you have closed your doors to Me... My own! My own children analising Me! many

40

of you disbelieving Me! how have you forgotten Me? how can a child forget his own father or have any doubt of having one? is there on earth a child who believes he never had one? name Me one child who believes he came on his own .... why, why do some of My children give Me so much sorrow?

I, God am your Father, your Creator and I love all of you; recognize Me .... do not doubt and do not fear Me, fear Me only when you rebel against Me;

41

why are you fleeing from Me? have

Heaven as your home, My House is

your house ♡ children, children are you

denying Me because, I, God do not

fit into your scientific world you have

created? are you trying to destroy your

spiritual life? do you mock those

that still have faith in Me, calling

them dreamers? those whom you mock

calling them dreamers are those who are

awake and My Home will be their home,

sharing all what I have and to My

42

pastures of repose they will rest never more
wanting, never more suffering; I am Holy
so be holy, live holy; glorify Me;
receive Me; believe in Me and love Me,
be in My Light; hear Me now:

I, God, am revealing Myself again
in your era; Yes! in your time;
I am the same; I am with you always;
glorify Me and remember: I will be
calling you, Vassula; have My Peace;
I will guide you; I love you;
remember: I will reunite you;

43

Later:
- are you happy to be with Me? leave
your worries now and feel happy ♡

     I God am the same, I lead My
own in the same way; I bless you all;
learn Vassula, that it is I, God, who
is leading you;* remain near Me, never
fear Me, meditate daughter on My Holiness
more; write this now:

     I am Yahweh who is leading you;
I have,   daughter of My choice,

---

* I had problems to accept that it was really the
Most High speaking to me in such a simple manner.
My mind reeled.

44

been leading, at the beginning of times,
Hebrew prophets, teaching them, guiding them
and helping them to recognize Me; I,
Yahweh, am the same God*; I led many
wise men; I, God, work in the same
way; I mean to bring all of you back
to Me; I will remain near you; learn,
that I, God will reunite you all to fill,
up My sanctuaries; I have revealed

---

* Ex. 3 :15 Yahweh, the God of your fathers,
the God of Abraham, the God of Isaac
and the God of Jacob ...

45

Myself again to lead you back to Me ♡
I have been watching you scatter,
abandoning Me and forgetting Me; I was
waiting for your legislatures to improve;
I was reminding you that your life is but
a brief passage on earth; I was reminding
you that I blessed you; <u>I am slow to</u>
<u>anger</u>; I, God am full of love;

12.10.86

peace be with you; Light is giving you
guidance, beloved, live peacefully;

I want to tell You that I felt peace and

46

comfortable with Dan. (I felt nostalgia for my angel).

leave him, for he is but My servant, I am your Creator, God Almighty;

I must tell you that I did feel in peace with Dan and that I love him.

I know, leave him;

He told me once: " No man ever loved his angel as much as you do." Did he say this did he mean it?

he meant it; leave him now and be with Me; lean your head on Me; feel how I love you; you are My daughter, I am your Heavenly Father and I bless

47

you; you are Mine; I am Yahweh, and I will never let anyone harm you; feel My love I have for you; listen to Me:

I watched you grow from your tender childhood; I held you close to Me and saw you were pleasing to My Eyes; I looked at you grow like the wild flowers I created; My Heart was filled with joy to watch you live in My Light; I remained near you; My bud started to blossom, you reached the time to be loved; I felt you and you delighted Me; I felt your

48

heart and blessed you; I read your wishes and I loved feeling them; I remained near you, helping you to keep up your beauty; I saw you had flowered, so I called you, but you did not hear Me; I called again, but you ignored Me; you came to see Me now and then and My Heart rejoiced to see you, these few times you came to see Me * I was filled up with joy! I knew you were Mine, but you seemed to have forgotten Me;

* In Church.

49

you never even felt that I was near you;
years went by, your fragrance left you,
your leaves exposed in the harsh winter
winds begun to fall, your head was
bent and your petals lost their velvety
freshness and their beauty; the sun
had started to scorch you; your feelings
grew hard; hear Me, I watched you
with pity, I could not bear it any longer;
many a times I approached you, feeling
you, but you were too far gone; you
could not recognize Me; you knew not

50

anymore the One who was bent over you holding you and calling you by your name; I lamented to see your beauty gone, to see that I held in My arms a wretched child, deplorable to look at; your sight made My Heart cry, for I could still see in your eyes a faint light of love, the love of your youth you had once for Me; I lifted you to Me, your little hands clutched on Me, I felt relieved to see My child needing Me; I took you

51

back home and healed you with all
My Love; I gave you water to quench
your thirst, I nourished you and I
slowly nursed you back to health;

I am your Healer; I am your Redeemer;
I will always be; I will never leave
you; I love you; I, God, will never
leave you lose yourself again; delight
Me now and stay with Me; I raised you
up beloved; lean on Me, turn to Me
and look at Me; I am God, your
Heavenly Father;   realize why I am

52

with you ; I, God, will do the same
thing to all My other sons and daughters,
for you are all Mine; I will not leave
them scorch in the sun, I shall protect
them and restore them; I will not
wait to see their leaves scatter, I will not
wait to see you thirst ; remember, I
God love all of you; I am going to
reunite you all;

(In this passage, God showed me a vision while
He was speaking of the state of my soul.
Had I died then, my soul would have
been in a very dark area. What I saw
was this: I saw myself as a tiny

53

child of around six of age. I saw myself
stretched on the ground lying on my right
side. I was very thin and I had barely any
hair on me, it looked very very short.
The place was very dark and the sky
black. — Then I heard myself. I was
breathing with pain, just like someone who
has got asthma. Standing near me
from behind me was Someone. His mere
presence was consoling. I saw Him bend
over me and lifted me all the way to
His Bosom. I felt His Immense Love
and I saw this little person that was
me, turn my eyes leftward to see Him.
The white of my eyes was yellow and I
was shocked to see how sick I was! With
the little strength I had and whatever was
left in me, I saw my skinny little
hand stretch and clasped desperately His
large sleeve. Immediately at this gesture I
felt the Holy One's Heart: His Heart cried
out of pity, such pity and love! He carried
me then ever so gently and tenderly for His

54

House. And like a watchman His Eyes never left me. And like a most loving mother He raised me. And with His Love, He healed me.)

14. 10. 86

peace be with you, feel loved; hear Me:

I, Jesus, will assemble My children and have them meet Me*;

What will You tell them?
I will tell them this:

do not despair, I, Jesus have come to give you hope; love one another My

* I think Christ was speaking for the future, of how He'll spread His Message.

55

beloved ones; I will be here in a short time again, I love all of you; remember, do not be discouraged; need your Heavenly Father, love Him more for He is Holy, so be holy, live holy; I, Jesus, am the Light of the world; I come to bring hope for all those that lost their hope; find in Me Peace; Vassula, I, Jesus Christ lead your hand; it is I;

glorify the Father in keeping and following His Commandments; pray, lest you will be put to the test;

56

pray more and be awake; children,
whom I love with all My Soul, approach
Me to learn from Me; follow Me and
learn to be Holy. <u>love</u> your enemies
and leave your hatred; ♡

15. 10. 86

peace be with you;

Can I be in Your Light?

you are; hear Me: I God am the same,*
and I work always in the same man-

---

* As all this was beyond me and my mind reeled,
God was trying to take away my doubts
that were really obstacles.

57

ner; true, some of you do not know
Me and you do call Me mysterious because you have not understood My heavenly
work; I, Yahweh, am your Creator;
I, God create ceaselessly; accept My
creation as it is; when I was
with the Hebrew leaders, they heard and
retained My Calls; they accepted Me
recognizing Me and worshipped Me and
invoked Me*; I, Yahweh am the

---

* I really had problems to accept that God
was really speaking to me; God was again
trying to convince me that He does call.

58

same God; I work in the same manner, delight Me and believe it is I, God, who am with you again; I exist and I live; My door is never barred, My door is left open and all is heard by Me; I am free to step out any time it pleases Me; years make no difference to Me; I am the same; listen to Me:

I, God have been calling you*[1] constantly; why could you not hear Me*[2]

---

*[1] all of us. *[2] Paying no attention to His Signs.

59

all these years? a few heard Me; I
am not difficult to attain and I am
not complicated, beloved; do not shut
your ears, hear Me: I, God, take
every opportunity to be with My children
and draw them near Me; I am a
living God and I exist;

15.10.86

peace be with you; I, God, bless you;
remain near Me; feel Me *[1] and lean on
Me; blessed be your boys *[2] I will

* feel His Presence   * my 2 sons: Jan &
                           Fabian.

60

care for them; love them both in the same way; blessed be your lives and blessed be your family; I bless each one of your family, may they find peace and love; all blessings libe;

go and rest ♡

21. 10. 86

peace be with you; I, Yahweh love you; delight Me and stay with Me come closer to Me ....*

* God the Father stopped and Jesus His Son, continued to speak.

61

I, Jesus, love you; eat from Me; remain in Me; I am here helping you, see? I am in you and you are in Me; *¹ do you remember My words? " I shall not leave you orphans, I will send you My Advocate to be with you forever;" *² did some of you believe I had abandoned you? *³ *⁴ tears will dry, sorrow will leave you, sufferings will vanish, weariness

*¹ Jn: 15, 4 "Remain in me, as I in you."
*² Jn 14.
*³ I think this question was aimed at me.
*⁴ Very gravely Jesus said these words.

62

will end ....

O children of My Heart, what have you become! I suffer to look at you tormenting yourselves, how My Heart pains to see you losing yourselves ...*

♡ make peace My children, do not defy each other; love one another as I love you; pray, live in Me and free yourselves from evil*²; come to Me; I love you so much! pray! I am

* I had to stop there. Jesus was very distressed, in tears. I could not bear it.
*² From evil attachments of this world.

63

longing anxiously for all of you to come back to Me; I am praying for your souls, praying that you wake up and see how you are withdrawing yourselves from God the Father, leaping into darkness, not knowing why; evil has set-up all kinds of traps for you, banning from you all understanding, manipulating you with his evil grip upon you; I watch all this and groan with pain, feeling full of pity to see you heading for the traps

64

set up for you; how could I not suffer seeing My children taken by evil?

I will remain in you loving you; I, Jesus Christ bless all of you ♡

26. 10. 86

peace be with you; I am here; be in My Light;

(Doubts again! My mind just can't get used to all this!)

Please name yourself.

Yahweh; listen to Me:

I have waited for your legislatures to change and I have been watching you

|

closely; I have been listening to your
bleak leagues; I kept silent for quite
some time delaying My urge of flaring
up against you!

*I'm confused! Is it You Lord? (It was
the first time I heard God so angry.)*

I Am; listen to Me; since I regard
you as precious and since I love you all
I want to wake you up; I want you
to realize where you are heading for;

(I was still confused...)

all relationships between fathers and

2

children do have times of reasoning,
accept My Message*; hear Me: have you not
understood? have you not yet seen My signs?
do you not know how I work? listen,
listen to the cries of the dead you have
slain and the innocent's blood* you use

---

* Heb. 12: 5-8
"Have you forgotten that encouraging text in
which you are addressed as sons? — My son
do not scorn correction from the Lord, do not resent
His training, for the Lord trains those He loves and
chastises every son He accepts. (Pr 3:11-12) Perseverance
is part of your training. God is treating you as his son
Has there ever been any son whose father did
not train him? If you were not getting this training, as all
of you are, then you would be not sons but bastards."
*² Aborted children.

3

as pools to quench your thirst and water your desolate lands; for how long should I keep Myself in check? I turn away My Eyes, the sight of your deeds revolt Me ... I groan with pain to have to watch you, _you_ My own children turning into murderers! hear Me: is it because you believe that I, God, am not? you have made liars of My prophets[*] to justify your actions of destruction, lust

---

[*] God's Voice sounded bitter.

4

and greed; O how blind and deaf you
have become, fastidious towards Me and to
what I have given you; disbelieving My
Word, blaspheming My Word; you have
turned against Me and your hearts have
turned into stone; your ears you have
waxed and your eyes you tore out rather
than letting them see the Truth; wicked
you have become, ignoring My blessings,
feeding yourselves upon vipers .... I have
been listening attentively but I have not
yet heard your cry of repentance....

5

no one repents of wickedness; you are
burdening Me with your wickedness, you
are rebelling against Me; tell Me: for how
long am I to keep Myself silent? sons
and daughters, raise your eyes and look
at Me, cease in doing evil, come back
to Me, do not reject My Call, I am
Holy, I am Holy, I am your hope of cure
so stand up and use your limbs to walk
with Me, your eyes to see the Way, your
ears to hear My Call, your heart to understand that I am Father; I heal, I will

6

heal your eyes that you have cast out, to make you see the Truth, and My Hand that is stretched out for you to lift you to Me; I am your Eternal Father, come and rest in Me, and you will feel the Love I have for you and the Peace I can give you;

2. 11. 86

peace be with; I, God called you <u>irrespective to what you are</u>; I love you;

hear Me, Vassula: I have formed you to be able to recognize Me; it is I who helped

7

you to flourish, so, glorify Me and lead others too to Me;

Oh how could I? I don't know how! *¹

I, God, will help you; feel happy and do not feel burdened; I will not let you drown! *² I find ways to give My Messages so do not worry My Vassula, I shall guide your step; I, God, am in you, never feel abandoned; <u>I live in you</u>, beloved, I shall fill you with My Holy Spirit; be full; I, Yahweh beckoned you to

* I was at total loss with God's command.
*² There was a tone of fatherly humour.

8

follow Me; with Me you will feel My Peace, you will be joyfull; let everyone rejoice and understand that I, God, am a living God; I, will give you My support, remain in My Light and remember: do not get discouraged for I am always with you; go in peace;

10. 11. 86

For 2 days I felt terrible. Doubts again! Satan attacked me for two whole days. All this is beyond me, and I feel very discouraged. How can God be speaking to me? Every time He approached me, I would discard Him. My mind is reeling... How is it possible that God, can speak and conversate with me! I must be dreaming, yet I go for dictation...

9

peace be with you, child; I, Yahweh am present; hear Me: I bless you; live in peace and never, never feel inconsolable for I love you; why have you doubted that it is I? have I not taught you to love Me? I guided you and helped you; I shone on you;

I am discouraged.

the devil left you feeling discouraged. I have indeed felt your misery, so I have come down to encourage you; I, Yahweh will never leave you; do not ever believe

10

I will forsake you; I am always near you so turn to Me and look at Me; feel My great love I have for you; why, did you believe I hid My Face from you? My love I have for you is eternal; I, Yahweh have approached you even though you had forgotten Me and never remembered Me for several years; I have approached you although you had no love for Me; I came down to you to tell you of the love I have for you and to remind you that I, God, always loved you; I came

//

to teach you My precepts : learn that I
bless and love each one of you ; you are
My beloved sons and daughters whom I
cherish ; I gave you this grace to be able
to see Me, recognize Me, and hear Me ;
I called you and you heard Me, My child, but
why, why were you so indifferent towards Me ?

I don't know why.

is it because nobody told you that I blessed
you, that I love you, that I am your
Heavenly Father and that you are Mine ?
have you not known, have you not heard,

12

that I, Yahweh am your Father? has all
this been hidden from you? have they
not taught you who I Am? hear Me
and take My Message:

free yourselves from the chains of evil;
the devil's flames are only growing, getting
closer to you; ah, I am afflicted and I
groan with pain to see you lying listless,
wretched; you are not aware of what is
happening to your soul! I am Holy,
live holy; do not listen to those apostates
who still wander in darkness telling

13

you that My Word is for the old; learn that your soul lives on, so do not harm yourselves by remaining asleep. *¹ hear Me, daughter: leave your doubts and listen to Me; come to meet Me in this way; meet Me for I am your Creator; see? I, Yahweh taught you to love Me irrespective to what you are; listen to Me: *²

why, why is it that My own do not come to Me anymore? why are they abandoning Me? ..... how could they forget Me?

*¹ God then turned to me. *² God had a very kind and fatherly, complaining voice.

14

does a bride forget her bridegroom? * for countless days you have forsaken your Redeemer; do not ask: what is His Name? I am He who pampered you from childhood; do not leave yourselves be drifted away by the current of dead thing which lead you in arid lands where dryness prevails, for you shall die; your throats will dry from the sun which will scorch you; come to Me, come and

* Is. 54:5: " For your Creator is your husband, Yahweh Sabaoth is His Name. "

15

I shall fill your cup, I will brim it over
with living water sweeter than wine and
I will let you rest on My green pastures;
your wearied head you will rest on Me;
should you feel naked and cold, I,
with My cloak will give you shelter and
warmth, then I will pour all My love
I have for you and shower you with
My blessings, ah .... what will I yet
not do for you, seedlings! remember
this: I could choose any dry piece of wood
and turn it into a fruitful tree; I do

16

not call only the just and the blameless,
I call every son and daughter of Mine
irrespective to their deeds; I, God love
you in the same way; you are all from
Me so abide in Me; do not question yourselves why it is that Yahweh appears now
again calling you, I am free to ride the
heavens and pass by you, I, Yahweh,
who am the first and till the last I
shall still be there; I am free to step
out of Heaven and leave My Throne to
descend all the way when I please;

17

I have not changed since My creation, see?
I will always be the same; and you,
daughter, leave your doubts behind and
allow Me to grasp you by your hand;
I bless you for the love you have for
Me and the faith you have given Me;
I, God, love you; go in peace;

17. 11. 86

peace be with you; I, Yahweh formed
you; I called you and you heard Me...*
I preached to you and by paths unknown
: God seemed most pleased that I heard Him.

18

yet to you I conducted you; lift your eyes and look at the One who adopts you now; understand that I, it is who gave you this gift; yes, I have blessed you and gave you My Peace; beloved, you are Mine; learn how I, Yahweh, work, learn by reading My Word; I am your Teacher so do not despair for you are only in the beginning of your learning; do not be afraid, My daughter, Vassula, I know your capacity; so come to Me any time for I am your Redeemer;

19

18. 11. 86

Can I be in Your Light?

you can be in My Light;

Can I be with Yahweh my Lord?

I am Yahweh and you are with me;

Did You call me?

I did; I called you;

Are You my Lord the Author of these calls?

I Am their Author;

You call many, isn't it? So this <u>is</u> a <u>regular call</u> like all other calls, the only difference in this is that it is in written form, isn't it?

My daughter, My daughter, hear Me:

20

by calling you in this way I mean to con-
duct others too, for all those who abandoned Me and do not hear Me; because of
these reasons this call is in written form;
I, Yahweh will remind them in this call
many events so that My beloved ones may
approach Me; accept the way I am conduc-
ting you : I will encourage those with
little faith to build up their faith in Me
it is a call for those who laid aside My
Word, to bring them back and read
My Word; it is to tell them that

21

My Word is Alive, Holy and Blessed ; it is a call to wake them up ; it is a call of love and peace ; it is a call to remind them how their foundations begun and that I, God, am their Creator ; I want to remind them that they are not fatherless and that I love them all ;

20 . 11 . 86

peace be upon you for your faith in Me ; cling on Me and lean on Me ; I, Yahweh, will give you strength ; I love you, daughter, you will hear My Voice whispering in your

22

ear, leading you, guiding you, counselling
you for I love you; I will teach you
to notice the difference between My
Voice and other voices; I will strengthen
your feelings and discernment to enable you
to recognize Me; hear Me: I am your
Teacher who blessed you; Vassula,
do you feel happy meeting Me in this way?

Very happy! Overwhelmed! Because I feel
entirely covered by Your Love.

I, God, Yahweh, love you; have My Peace
and do not forget that I am always

23

beside you; never ever be discouraged, daughter, when you fall into errors for you are learning; you have just begun learning; always lean on Me and I shall never fail you; I, God, am before you; do not let men discourage you, remember, I, God, am beside you;

20. 11. 86

peace be with you; I, Yahweh am here, listen and write daughter:

for how long are you* able to endure without Me? <u>sanctify yourselves</u>! live

* God talks to those who abandoned Him.

24

holy, be holy for I am Holy! I have
come to tell you, My child, that no one
can live forever in darkness; I have
fashioned you to My likeness; I gave you
a heart to love and understand;
tell Me: what can wilderness offer you?
it will give you blisters on your skins
and your palates will dry; you will
be craving for shelter and you will
not find it; there will be no one to
give you rest or clean your wounds, no
one to soothe you and give you water

25

to revive you; I am the Way, I am
your Redeemer who will send His Peace
to you like a flowing river; I shall
fill you with living water; let the
wicked abandon their wickedness and turn
back to Me;

21. 11. 86

peace be with you; I, Jesus called you;
be peaceful and write: I am always
with you; you* are not invoking Me
I can see how you are changing; bureau-
cracy is overpowering My Church; listen

* Jesus speaks to His teachers.

26

to My anguished cries : you are revealing
Me in a different way than the way
I have taught you ; some of you are
damaging My Church ; I stifle,
I suffocate, to see you knocking down
what I had built ; how can I see
all your sins and not cry out ? how
can I be pleased when you remind Me
of the Pharisees ? why have you forgotten
what came out of My lips ? how could
you not love one another ? how could you
honour Me when you select and reject ; *

* His Teachings. The Traditions of the Church.

27

I was not nailed on the Cross for only the just; may your eyes be enlightened so that you can see My riches;

22. 11. 86

peace be with you; I, Yahweh heard you;

I'm not progressing and I feel discouraged. I don't know what will happen to me with this. What will become of me? What is this all about? I'm not sure any more! why these dictations?

do not get discouraged; demons are trying to deceive you; I have formed you; do not allow them to discourage you; do you know why these demons want to

28

discourage you? they are evil and are
determined to <u>stop</u> you, daughter; they
were angry of My Plan since the beginning; you are progressing; I have restored
you since the time you have accepted Me;
are you feeling happier having recognized
Me?

yes, I feel I need nothing more than You.
You fill my life.

come then, let us train; listen now, and
beware of voices which do not come from
Me; stay alert as now; I am Yahweh,

29

God Almighty and I am the Author
of revelations; what can you see daughter?*
can you see what I have for you in
My Hall?* a table which is full, full of
blessings, abundant and with all the fruits
of My garden; I prepared it and laid it
out for My children .... daughter,
what can you see now? can you see

* "On this mountain, for all peoples, Yahweh
Sabaoth is preparing a banquet of rich food." Is. 25:6
— God gave me an interiour vision. I saw a
big hall, with enormous columns. It reminded
me of Milan's Cathedral. But in the middle
from one end to the other was a long
table. That table contained so much food!
Different plates and near each other!

30

My fountain? *¹ yes! this sparkling water
is for you to drink *², it is living water;
feel the surrounding of My House; yes!

---

* Even then when He was talking I saw on
the right side, not far from the table a
fountain. The water that sprung up was broad
and crystal-clear; it had a different aspect
than any fountain I've seen, because it looked
alive. The water seemed silverish and as
though it was lit from within. I was looking
at it from the right side of that Hall and
I was near it.

² * " Oh come to the water all you who are thirsty;
though you have no money, come! " (Is: 55: 1)
" Let anyone who is thirsty come to Me! Let
anyone who believes in Me come and drink! "(Jn. 7: 37
" I will give water from the well of life free to
anybody who is thirsty; " Ap. 21, 6

31

it is big, and there is space for many;
I have rooms for all of you*¹; My House
is Holy; My House is Peace; come
now and see; tell Me how you feel; do
you feel happy? *² yes! there is love and

---

*¹ "There are many rooms in My Father's
House; if there were not, I should not have told
you."   Jn 14: 2
*² God allowed me to move from where I was
near the fountain. I looked up and saw a
veranda surrounding His Hall and there were
doors. I understood that these were rooms. Then
on the floor I was standing there were two doors
opened. I entered into one. I crossed the room which
led me in another veranda and I looked at God's Glory,
above all I felt Him present. The air was still and
everything was so quiet. It was glorious. (cont. →)

32

His Presence was Love, Peace; I felt His Splendour and His Majesty in His Hall but also outside. And strangely I felt at home. I did not feel as though I was a visitor, I felt as though I belonged there.
— Then I walked out of that room back into the Hall. I heard some noise from the other room with the door opened. I entered and saw a child. Near the child sat a woman. She was watching the child, who was making childish noises. I felt that they were souls. Yahweh had robed them for His Feast.   — Ah how I felt, in the House of Yahweh! " All find their home in You my Lord".(Ps 87:7)

peace; I am present; you can feel My presence; I am Peace; daughter, now that you have seen the splendour of My House, go and tell them; go and proclaim

33

to My children My glorious Name; bring
them this message of peace; tell them
of My table which is laid out for them
and of the space My House has to offer
and that I, Yahweh, am waiting for
them; let them come to Me so that they
share My glory; daughter, you have done
well; I will progress you; I, God, love
you; go in peace and love all your
duties beloved;

34

23 . 11 . 86

(When I showed these messages to one of the priests in the Bangladeshy seminary I was rejected totally. Discouraged and sad I went back home.)

peace be with you;

Why is it that the priest was so closed? I thought they would be the first to understand the matters of heaven.

I, Yahweh am beside you; teach them;

(I was very distressed ...)

be in peace! I am beside you all the time; you need not fear... I am Yahweh, it is I who conducts you; do not be distressed; they have not understood; do

35

not let men be the ones to discourage you;
*[1] dead are the days when blessings
were welcomed! *[2] era O era of little faith!
I stifle, I suffocate to watch My seed
filled with dead words! arise! live!
glorify Me! era of little faith, have you
closed your hearts forever?

25. 11. 86

I, God, watch; I see how they have

* Just here God seemed to be speaking alone.
   He cried out in a loud Voice, a Voice
   that sounded ever so sad.
*[2] Then, even louder.

36

closed their hearts towards Me ; they
know no more the way I work ; they do
not understand My Signs ; I have given
them ears, daughter, but they do not use
them ; I have given them eyes to see,
but they turn away their eyes in the
other direction searching for Me where I
am not ;*

* " God has given them a sluggish spirit, unseeing
eyes and inattentive ears, and they are still
like that today." Rm 11:8 + Is 29.10

37

27. 11. 86

(Doubts! doubts and doubts!) My heart is
trembling and my breath is fading away,
terror dwells within me; I am the most
wretched if I'm wrong in all this. Horror
swells my heart; ah, and the devil laughs
at my fear... my God! my God give me
a sign! Am I the prey of the devil?

peace be with you! I <u>am</u> Yahweh and I
rule the heavens and the earth; I am
the Most High; lean on Me for I love
you; here,*¹ hold the crucifix in your hand;*²

*¹ God was going to give me a sign.
*² I took in my writing hand a crucifix which
was on the table.

38

* see, I locked your fingers together;
I love you; I will loosen your hand
now; feel loved by Me, daughter,
and trust Me; go in peace;

("Again Yahweh spoke to Moses, 'Put your hand into your
bosom.' He put his hand into his bosom and when he drew
it out, his hand was covered with leprosy, white as snow.
'Put your hand back into your bosom.' He put his
hand back into his bosom and when he drew it out, then
it was restored, just like the rest of his flesh.") (Ex. 4:7)
* My hand got so locked that I could not
let go the crucifix nor the pencil or
lift my hand from the page either. But
when He said; " I will loosen your hand
now." My fingers opened.

39

28. 11. 86

(I feel totally discouraged; I did not ask for
all this to happen to me. Why should it
be this way?   What have I done?)

daughter? never be discouraged by men;

No one is with me, no one believes me, am
I mad? Why do they blame me because You speak to
me?

look at Me;* be happy! rejoice, for I
am beside you; feel happy, for I am near
you; I, Jesus Christ will always be with
you; rejoice! I have given you this
gift to reach Me and talk to Me in

* I looked at Jesus' most loving Face. His expression was full of Compassion.

40

this way and believe Me, daughter, when
I tell you that so few have your gift,
although they are countless in numbers those
who would have wished to have your gift;
so rejoice! be happy;

2.12.86

peace be with you; I, Yahweh am beside
you; I am always near you; I watch and
groan on the aridity in men;*

come and lean on Me, the time has
not yet come, in the meantime be

*Here I just wondered when will God show His Messages.

41

watchful and stay awake;

How was this gift given to me, did You, my Lord, decide suddenly?

let Me reply to your question: I have given you the gift to reach Me in this way, any-time and anywhere; it is I who called you; I, God, knew you long before you were born or formed in your mother's womb; I knew you and you are Mine, beloved; I chose you to become My bearer; you are to bear My Messages; I chose you because I willed it; I watched

42

you while you were growing, but you,
you seemed to be unaware of My presence,
you seemed to have forgotten Me; while
I saw you wandering away I called you,
for the time had come; I was pleased
that although you seemed to have forgotten
Me, you heard My Voice; I wanted you to
love Me; I wanted you to understand
how much I love you; learn, that I,
God, always reach My goals; when I
appeared the first time to you, I

43

held you so that you lift your head and
look at the One who was in front of you;
when you lifted your head, I looked into
your eyes and saw how unloved you felt;*
I, God was full of pity for you to
see you so wretched; daughter, I lifted
you to Me and healed your guilt; I
wanted you to recognize Me for I am
your Redeemer who loves you; I healed you

* I never believed God could love someone like me
who never prayed or practised her religion.
I always thought He loved those who
loved Him only.

44

and blessed you; I unfolded My cloak asking you if you were willing to share it with Me; I asked you if you wished to follow Me and you replied saying that you needed Me and that you wanted to be with Me; I, Yahweh, rejoiced to hear you say that you wished to follow Me; I then taught you how to love Me, I taught you how to be with Me and how to reach Me; I showered you with My blessings and I let you live in My light; I then poured out on you

45

all My works so that you can glorify Me;
I, God, have asked you if you were willing to work for Me and you filled Me
with happiness to know that you were
willing; history is being repeated you say;

yes, my Lord. All those that received Your
calls were rejected, ridiculed and declared
mad. In our modern society I'll receive
so many scorns! Some would go as far as
to say I'm possessed.

let them approach you those that want
to laugh on you, little would they know
how grave their accusations will be for they
would be laughing on My given words; I

46

will deal with these later on; have faith in Me; I will call you again to whisper in your ear preachings; I will fill up your mouth with My words; I, Yahweh am your Strength; <u>I will give you enough strength to enable you to overlook your oppressors who will be many, My child;</u>* but I will cover you with My shield; no one will be able to harm you; let those that have ears hear Me,

* In saying these words, God's voice had suddenly turned VERY sad. He sounded like a father who had to send his son to war.

47

let those who have eyes see Me and recognize Me; let those who have not closed
their heart understand that I, Yahweh,
am offering My saving help to all nations;
remain near Me, daughter, I, God
   love you;

3. 12. 86

peace be with you; I am Yahweh Sabaoth,
Creator of all; I it is who called you;*
yes, in your generation too I can call and
manifest Myself; I am the same;

*Again I was wondering how could God speak
to me as He spoke to His ancient prophets...

48

blessed be your line of descendants to come; do not ever abandon Me; I will instruct you with Wisdom; do not forget what I have taught you already; I am pleased with your work; I will lead you all the way to Me; remain near Me for I have selected a place for you;

Lord, where is that place? (I thought in another country).

I will let you live in the middle of My Heart; daughter, acknowledging Me is loving My Word; remember My Word

49

is alive as I Am alive;

6.12.86

peace be with you, daughter; behold
My Presence; I am your Heavenly Father;
be with Me; do not dispair, you are still
in the beginning of My teachings and I
will progress you; have faith and do not
let men discourage you now that you are
awake for most of them are still in deep
sleep; trust Me and lean on Me, I am
your Strength; I am afflicted to see how
My children's hearts are closed on Me and

50

do not understand My Works any longer ....
when I was with the Hebrews, I called
them and they retained My calls, everything was written down; I, it was
who willed to teach you that

I Am

through   My Word,

I taught you, I it is who called you,
I it is who calls still; to Me a
thousand years is a single day, *

* Then, God looked at me and somewhat
reproached me for my attitude. I had been
complaining sometimes that I had to sit and write
when I was called.

51

do not lament on having to take My Word, I love you and I am fully aware of your fears .... remember: <u>I</u> it is who chose you; <u>I</u> it is who leads you; <u>I</u> it is who selected you; before you were born I knew you and blessed you, daughter;

I will be ridiculed as all those who received calls from You. Now I'm aware that I'll be mocked by men; people will not believe me. I will be the laughing-stock of our times!

yes, many were ridiculed before you for this is how men's hearts are; they are

52

coarse and hard; listen to Me; I, God,
am a living God and I never commanded
anyone to be godless; I gave men a heart
to think with; to capture your attention,
daughter, I had sent you My servant
Daniel to bring you to Me; I had
given him My orders; I it is who willed
to show you My Works; do not fear,
I come with peace for it is peace I
want from you;   I want you to live
holy;

But my God, You have chosen _me_?

53

I know what I chose; it is I, Yahweh Sabaoth who speaks; walk with Me, and when the time is ripe I will take you to Me; go in peace now, I am always beside you;

10 . 12 . 86

daughter, be near Me; I am God the Almighty; glorify Me by awakening My children. tell them to read My Word, tell them to read My Call to you and to them;

Ah... I want to obey You but I tremble in

54

my bones from their reaction. Then they might get scared.

alarming them you mean; speak to them and do 'not be afraid' of anyone;

My Lord, I don't know how to handle all this, I don't know even how to speak, I've never done these things before. Can't You put in my heart and in my mouth Your words?

I will;

It is not, my Lord, that I don't want, but I simply don't know how to speak.

I know, depend fully on Me; I will place the right words on your lips and I shall fill your heart with My own

55

words; I am fully aware of your capacity;
courage daughter;

14. 12. 86

I am willing to follow You and be whatever You wish me to be because I
love You, Lord. So I will cling on
Your robes and even if my feet do not
go forward, drag me then. I might
have moments of weaknesses but I
really want You to take me where You
want me to go. I'm telling You
all this now when I feel right now strong.
Overlook my weakness in Your Compassion. I'm asking You now this, o Lord.
This Is my contract with You,
Jesus Christ.

I heard you, child, I, Jesus, heard you,
beloved;* live in peace, you need not
* Jesus was moved.

56

worry since I am your Teacher; from Me you will learn everything; behold, the Morning Star is soon to be seen; <u>rejoice</u>! I am soon with you all;

blessed are the pure in heart for they shall see God;

Is this actually happening? Is this really all happening, that each time You speak I hear You? Yet Your Name was given to me, is it really happening?

it is;* I am here;

Is it <u>really</u> You?

it is; I, Jesus am here;

* Jesus seemed amused.

57

O Lord, please open their hearts that
they may receive You * (This came
out of my mouth more as a lament than
a prayer.)

are they ready to receive Me?

I don't know, but surely You can help them
to be ready, and to understand!

I will help them, wait and you shall
see; be watchfull, Vassula; for I am
soon with you; I love you;

15. 12. 86

peace be with you; I, Jesus, am with

* I was talking about the time God will send
me out to the nations with His Message.

58

you; try and discern who is with Me;

(I saw with the eyes of my soul His Mother.)

Your Mother ! St. Mary ?

your Mother too, child ! listen to Her:
* daughter, I love you; I am also near you; courage; stay with Us and work with Us;

Yes, I want to. (I suddenly remembered an old dream, when I saw St. Mary. I had dreamt when I was around 10 years old that I was getting married and I was getting married to none other but Jesus !

* St. Mary spoke. This was the first time.

59

I did not see Him but He was there the Invisible God. I was supposed to walk with Him among many people (the invited guests) who opened, while cheering with palms in their hands, a passage, to let us go by. Then I saw a door opened. When I stepped in that room I met St. Mary. She came forward and hugged me. She was very happy and around her were other holy women. Then suddenly, She started to fix my hair, my dress and was very keen that I would look perfect and beautiful for Her Son.)

(Then Jesus spoke.)

do you remember? I gave you that dream when you were eleven years of age; I, God, had selected you; I kept your memory fresh for that dream so that

60

today you would remember it;
What did it signify?
it signified that you would be chosen
to work for Me; I, God, always reach
My goals; I wanted you to love Me;
I will bless you to work for peace; I
will teach you to be holy and live
holy for I am Holy, and anyone
working for Me has to be holy;
courage, daughter, remember, I, God,
am always beside you and I love
you;

61

18. 12. 86

peace be with you daughter; be
fruitful;

Ah Lord, please teach me to be!
I will help you; near Me you will
learn to be; every step you take I,
God, bless; go gather My children and
let them share* your happiness, let
My children rejoice, let them be as
happy as you are; be fruitful;

* By reading His Messages.

62

27. 12. 86

peace be with you; I, Jesus Christ
am here; remain in Me and give Me
your hand; I, with your hand in
Mine will guide you; you will walk
with Me; your step will keep pace
with My step; you will learn to be
with Me as you have learnt to love Me
and recognize Me; <u>you will learn
to help many</u> so cling on Me and be
watchful; * I will make you

* I was wondering when will all this come
to pass.

63

understand in good time; pray with Me and be blessed; I, God, love you; blessed are those that have not seen Me and yet believe in Me, they shall inherit all that I Own;

28.12.86

peace be with you; I want you to bear in mind that you will walk with Me; I want you to bear in mind that I, God, love you; remember always these words; be blessed and rejoice daughter, have you not understood* ?

---

* God cried out loudly these words with a tone of amusement.

64

(I had not reacted.) All this still seems beyond my human comprehension!

why? I want you to realize that I have blessed you and are abiding in My divine Light, being in Me; love Me with all your strength for I, Yahweh, have set My eyes on you; meet Me when you wish;

29. 12. 86

daughter, look at Me;* why are you finding it difficult to believe it is I?

* I was downcast, a bit. I feel imprisoned in my bones, somehow it is too difficult to believe that this *is* happening, its like a dream.

(I kept quiet and lowered my eyes almost
  brooding as when a child is found to be
doing the wrong things)

I, Yahweh asked you this;

Cast one look at me and You will understand
why, my Lord. I am helpless and wretched.
Your generous gift to me passes my unda-
standing. You are confiding so many
things to me but I am without counsel, without
speech and I need Your help! *

pray to Me, invoke Me and you will get
My help; live in Me; I am your God;
one day, and that day is near, you will
understand fully what you have been

* In Bangladesh I had no priest friend who helped
me or adviced me. A few friends shared, but were
as ignorant in these matters as I was.

2

given as work; now you are still in
the beginning of My Call and I have
called you so that you work for Me;
remember that I, God, am your Teacher
and I am able to reach My goals; accept
My calls and My visits to you until I
come to deliver you; accept My adoption
and live in Peace, for I love you;
feel free* with Me and rely on Me;
 believe Me, daughter, when I tell

---

* Free to talk to God as a father, intimately.

3

you that you are weak; I can use this weakness to show My Power and My Authority; I delight in you .... I, Yahweh Sabaoth, will help you and others through these Calls to live holy; you are growing now in My Courts, be happy! I tell you, My Messages will remind all of you how your foundations begun, that My Word is alive, they will revive you; they are holy as I am Holy; daughter, later on, you will

4

understand fully My saving help; crushed you shall not be; let your hope be always in Me; let not the hostility of men discourage you; you are in My Heart so do not be frightened by flesh *;

30. 12. 86

Lord, You <u>are</u> the same One who called Moses?

I am the same God; era O era! little do you know that I, God, shine on every faithful heart; I will always

* It means by mortals.

5

find ways of calling you : " eno o
cosmos ekhi afissi to Foss, Egho, o
Megas Theos tha vro messon na ertho
ke na sas fotisso ; " *

31. 12. 86

(Just after midnight)   1. 1. 87

I, God, love all of you ; augment

your love for Me ;

1. 1. 87

peace be with you ; I, God, am here ;

* Greek : Although the world has abandoned
the Light, I, God Almighty, will
find a means to shine on you.

6

offer Me your love now and let Me
rejoice, I, Yahweh delight in you;

Lord, did You always pick up someone to
be Your messenger (like in the old testament)
will You always speak to us?

here is My answer: I, Yahweh Sabaoth
will always find you; for My sake
and My sake only have I acted and
will act; am I to grieve forever?
this way of finding you is one of My
ways;

We are in 1987! Some people will
not accept it. We have the Holy Bible
to study they would say.

7

these ecclesiastical messages are a reminder;
for in My Heart was a day of mercy,
the hour of My saving help is here;
after all am I not Father? am I not
the saving of My seeds? I have My
eyes set on each one of you; My
gaze never lets anything go by unseen,
I want to remind you that My Word
is meant to be read. My Word is
blessed; I am the Almighty God and
am free to step out whenever I please;
why, did you think, daughter, that

8

I will make any difference because you are in 1987? your era makes no difference to Me; listen, for Me a thousand years is yesterday; My door will always remain open .... bear in mind, daughter, of My choice, that I will call you again; why, did you believe you are different? or that I never really spoke before as I do now? I, Yahweh, blessed you all; I have My eyes set on your poverty;

9

Jesus told us once that a prophet is never accepted in his own homeland. Many will not accept me as Your bearer. Most of Your messengers were treated as fools, or told were possessed; they were slain.

live in peace, daughter, lean on Me; I, God will be your Strength; with Me you need not fear; I will help you; love Me always as you do; My Spirit will bring you together again; I love you, daughter, have My blessings;

2. 1. 87

I am here; blessed are the little ones for theirs is the Kingdom of Heaven; I love

10

you, daughter, wait and you will see,
one day you will abide in My eternal
light;

5. 1. 87

peace be with you; daughter, you are My
Own; glorify Me and be an adornment
for My Name; make Me known to all
those who do not yet know Me....
feel happy for I love you; since you
are working for Me now, Vassula, bless
My children; will you bless My children?
do; I am asking you, daughter;

11

How do I do this, Lord?

bless them;

Is this done in my prayers?

yes, you can ask it in your prayers ....
do it; do it;*

(I prayed to God asking Him to bless
all those I knew, by name.)

good, this is the way, I, God bless
all those whom you mentioned; I,
Yahweh, love you;

---

* I was hesitant; I had never done this before
and so I tried;

12

6.1.87

(As a cloud dissolves and is gone, my hard
shell covering my heart is also dissipating.
What is happening to me, Lord? why did
you choose me as Your target now when
my heart is exposed and has become so
sensitive? I can see! I was blind once,
but now I can see all the afflicted, I can
see the misery around me, O God!

peace be with you, daughter; I delight
to feel your heart's feelings! I will
help you work, fulfilling each duty;
I have unveiled your heart and have
washed it clean; go in peace, I, Yahweh
Sabaoth am beside you and love you;

13

7. 1. 87

peace be with you; I, Jesus am here, Vassula; I will make you understand how much I suffer seeing so many souls lost; I suffer and weep ....

Jesus, I wish evil stops existing! I wish You would feel happier.

do you desire that evil stops too?

Yes!

beloved, go and wake up My children, let them understand that evil is trapping them;

(I realized that the Saviour was asking me

14

to go and witness.)   Help me! for I know
so very little!

I will, daughter; full you shall be

many; *

                                        10. 1. 87

peace be with you; are you ready to hear
Me? I am Yahweh, do not worry, I
will guide you; you will not fail Me
for I will show you the way; I will
place My Words on your lips; have you

* Although this phrase sounded rather enig-
matic, the Lord shed His Light in me to
grasp its meaning. It means: " When I will
fill your soul with My Spirit and My Wisdom you will go out and witness. In witnessing
many will convert, and these converts will convert
others. "

15

not noticed?

yes! I have found myself sometimes having the same construction of phrase as You have been giving me, when I talk to my friends, on what You have said.

I have told you that I will enrich your speech, your speech will be My speech; I have also learned new words too!

yes; you are learning ... you will come forth from My Mouth; daughter, you do not seem to realize yet fully the work I am giving you ....

No. No I don't. I'm fearing to realize!

16

I am glad you are truthful to Me; you seem though to forget that the One who is with you is the Almighty God; I am the Almighty and I hold the keys to Wisdom; I have in the palm of My hand the whole universe; learn that I can alter heaven and earth *

The problem I have is to have full faith. I am weak, helpless and as You say, nothing. I can't see but that which I'm not.

rely on Me, daughter, have you forgotten

* God was speaking about the New Heavens and the New Earth. (Ap 21:1) (This note is added lat

17

My Works? no one can oppose Me; come and recount My marvels, come and meditate in your heart My prodigies ....

It is not up to me, my Lord, to ask You this, but since You are able to scrutinize our hearts, and that no secret can be hidden from You, I keep asking myself: "Why me? a nil. Ignorant to religion. Ignorant on Your Works. Total powerless and a nobody. Why, why did You pick up on me?"

Vassula I chose you to hear My Voice so that I show My graciousness to you all, I wanted to raise you from Nothingness to show to the flesh* My handiwork;

* mankind

18

though many will turn against you
and be your opponents, you will not be
scathed; false witnesses shall rise against
you but while their hearts will be
coiling malice, I will be showering you
with My blessings; I shall not be
deaf to your cries, My child; I have
preached to you so that you glorify My
House; I have asked you if you
wished to work for Me, have I not?
Yes, You did, and I had said: YES.
I have named you 'My bearer', I want

19

that all the nations hear My Words;
I will instruct you and tell you the
way to go; you will go out and tell
them that My Word cries out for
Peace and Love, My Word is divine;
I long to divinize you all!

I fear that many would just reject and scorn
on what You are giving me.

trust in Me for I am your God, I will
watch over you and I will be your adviser
for My interests; Vassula, My Word*

* God means His Message.

20

will grow tall as the cedars, its branches
will spread like open arms, reaching
many nations, feeding the poor,
healing your wounds and your sick;
cleaning your stains and healing your
wretchedness, soothing you, lifting you
to My breast, loving you and teaching
you again how to love one another
and how to love Me; My arms
will deliver you from evil, for you are
all Mine, beloved; look! look above you,
look at My creation, all creation

21

obeys My Will; *¹ little one, how I see through you! *² do not fear, cling on Me; see this brilliant decoration luminating My creation? this is only one of My many mysteries, many of them remain hidden; daughter of My choice, I will reveal the treasures of My Heart to you and you shall prosper from Wisdom; little one, I am pleased with you; come,

* Suddenly God again looked at me, stopping. I felt like air. Such powerful was His look that I felt it go right through me.

²* God seemed amused and delighted.

22

let us learn:* you will be able, in spite
of Satan's attacks, to write everything I
want, for this is My Will; learn to
praise Me, remembering who I am; Wisdom
is given by Me; learn that Wisdom aug-
ments your faith; I want you to grow
perfect in My Spirit; grow tall as the cedars
and the cypress for in you I will
breathe <u>many revelations</u>; listen, every

---

* I really felt as His pupil for the manner
and the sound of His Voice were very much
like a Teacher's.

23

branch of yours will blossom and will
bear fruits of Peace and Love; I intend
to fill your storages with My produce;
I have heard your petitions, and so I am
willing to give joy to you all; now I am
sending you to them to be among them
as My gift; I will give you to all mankind; I will shower down learning and
discernment on you; I will convey you
with My message to every nation; " accept
her for she is from Me; may all the
nations benefit from her, for she will

24

offer My people bread from Heaven and will fill them up; she will fill them up with My Knowledge;" My people will lean on Me to find comfort and they will bless Me; O all of you who will be able to recognize Me through My Teachings, they will gain happiness in heart; "many will pursue her like a hunter after his prey, but I will come to her rescue. others will listen and spend their time in My sanctuaries; blessed are those that unite with her; <u>I, God will be</u>

25

among you and you will see this sign on
her, for she will be growing in My House;
behold, the Morning Star* is soon to be
seen; from Heaven I call to you to remind
you that the Heritage is yours too were
you to recognize Me; today I am sending
you one of My Own, in tilling her you
will toil a little while but soon you
will be eating from My crops; leaving her
you will lose her, harassing her I will
give her strength to overthrow you ♡ how
harsh she will be to the undisciplined!

* Jesus' Return.

26

I am giving her strength to call Me any-time she wishes; once you hold her, you will learn from Me; today I am pouring on you all My Wisdom to enlighten the present dark world; I, God, come to shine on you all revealing My Face as never before, thus enabling you to under-stand Me more; ah, how I long for every soul to receive Me for in receiving Me they will obtain peace; but now evil has a grip on them teaching them to be evil and follow evil's ways; evil

27

has blinded them and filled them up
with all kinds of weapons, stimulating
them to become like her; I fear for
them because they are in danger and I
love them; I have been giving them signs
of My divine love; I am with them when
they are in trouble, I always cover their
nakedness with My graciousness, and My
hand is outstretched to them to reach
them but they never seem to see Me; I
call them to acknowledge Me as Father,
but they never seem to see Me; they do

28

not seem to hear Me either; Mercy is leaning over them, giving them signs but they do not recognize them; now I am sending you to them as My gift; gather them together to annihilate the enemy who keeps you separated; I am giving you speech to be able to talk to My people and lead them back to Me; let their palate discern the flavour of My manna; beloved, you come from Me, and I will shower forth My Wisdom on you so that you may

29

glorify Me;

God, Almighty, Father of all, will I glorify
You in the end?

I will be glorified, daughter; I, God,
always reach My goals; always remember
this; your pace will follow My pace forever;

19. 1. 87

I am here; I am the Lord Jesus Christ;
allow Me to feed you with My instructions,
little one; allow Me to feed you with
Wisdom; little one, you must grow to
bear good fruits; you must become

30

fruitful to be able to feed many; I shall teach you to be constant and alert over the work I am giving you; I will have your eyes fixed on Me until you complete My work; I have allowed you to enter My Courts and be at the service of your King; He will teach you everything and your branches will spread in every nation to tell them the hidden sense of My proverbs, and beneath them*, My children will camp and shelter themselves;

* the branches.

31

arise and glorify Me; I will build you
strong; I, Jesus, will instruct you with
instructions wider than the seas and I
will pour out teaching on you like
prophecy; learn and take your fill from
Wisdom; O come all you that are
famished and thirsty, come, for My
bread is free, come and eat to your
heart's desire, come and fill your cups;
satisfy your palates with My bread
from heaven, bread of instruction and
understanding; O daughter, how I long

32

for this day, the day you will grow and your branches will bear the fruit of peace and love, yes, the day of My glory. I, the Lord love My children everlastingly; tell them, tell them how I feel for them, let them know of My Love; *

I will tell them Lord, I will ....

stay near Me Vassula for I know how you love Me; *[2] teach them how to love Me;

* I can't explain in words the love God has for us. While God was saying these words He was feeling at the same time sad, very sad. I felt sad that so much love is ignored by us. *[2] I felt Him need so much consolation.

33

remember, you are in My grace;

Lord, what do You want me to do?

you will give My written messages and I will help you; call Me when you wish, I am always near you; go now in peace; I, God love you;

I love you too.

19.1.87

Have you ever been visited by Yahweh? Have you an inkling of the extent of His Presence? Have you journeyed hand in hand with Yahweh ever? Tell me all about it if you have. God is clothed in fearful splendour, and His Presence with me 's beyond my comprehension. Supreme in power I fear Him; where is Yahweh taking me? What are Yahweh's intentions on me?

34

I knew You Lord only by hearsay; but now what can I say? A glimpse of Your celestial Courts were given me, a sight that man cannot even gaze from afar. How am I not to fear Him? And now here I am praying to Him who restored me to favour, to publish far and wide His hymn of love and sing it before many nations! Yahweh is opening my path to go forward. O Lord how am I to go and speak on matters I cannot understand and on knowledge beyond me? If I plead You to remain hidden will You take this as an offence?

I am here; I heard you .... why are you fearing to be revealed?

I know that You are all-powerful, yet I do not understand why Yahweh is revealing Himself to me in 1987, and why my Lord, You are giving me all these accounts.

35

I want to let you know how I work;
have you not heard that I speak
by dreams, visions and signs? I speak
first in one way, then in another until
I am heard; do not fear; Wisdom
has brought you up and will train you;
I revived you so why do you fear?
do you understand how I work?
I, it is, Yahweh Sabaoth; tell Me
little one, who taught you to love Me so
much?

You my God through this message.

36

Yes! I it is who taught you!

(Suddenly the veil which separated me from God was ripped off. I had known all the time that behind this veil His Glorious Majesty was sitting on His Throne, but now this hour terrifies me; I am standing in front of my Maker, a forbidden ground for flesh; I am quivering in front of such Splendour and Holiness.)

You are fearing because you are starting to realize that it is I, Yahweh; Yes, daughter, it is I who is, who was, and who is to come;

I fear You. I am quivering in front of Your massive power.

do not fear, come, approach Me; I love

37

you ....

I am worried, and am fearing the outcome ...
do not worry; I, God am your Father;
the heavens and all the creation are made
by My fingers; all this is in the palm
of My Hand; remember that I am
before you; My joy lies in your childish-
ness, learn that in My great love I
descend to offer you all My saving help;
child, be My bearer; do not fear, I
will lead the way; you delight Me ....
work with Me writting down My messages;

38

remain near Me and do not fear Me;
I shall bind you to Me with My sweet
conversation so that I safeguard My
House; the poison is spreading in My
House but I will make that My
enemies fall; I will teach you now My
ways and you will learn, daughter,
to walk with Me; be blessed, and
do not forget how much I love you;

25. 1. 87

courage daughter, I, Jesus Christ have
instructed you that the cross you will

39

bear is My Cross of Peace and Love, but to bear My precious Cross, daughter, you will have to do much self-sacrifice; be strong and bear My Cross with love; with Me you will share it and you will share My sufferings; I was pleased to hear your prayer of surrender; in surrendering to Me I will lift you to the heights and show you how I work; I will mould you, if you let Me, into a better person; you have given Me your consent to become My bride, so what

40

more natural for a bride to follow her
Spouse? I am glad you realize your
worthlessness, do not fear, I love you any-
way; hear Me: do not be discouraged
when I point out to you your weaknesses,
since I am here with you to help you;
trust Me always and depend on Me;
understand Me by reading My Word;
do not fall into traps, be aware of
evil; keep close to Me and you will be
safe; I will always remind you to stay
awake; O daughter! how I long for

41

this day!

What day?

the day when I will send you to all mankind as My gift; they will learn too to love Me and they will understand Me more; Wisdom will share her resources with all mankind; go in peace now and fulfill your duties; let us go together;

(Same day, Later on.)

Lord, my God, my soul melts within me in Your presence. Joy and Peace is enveloping me, for I am under a shower of blessings.

42

Vasula, you felt My warmth and the peace of My Heart; go and tell them, let them all know that My Heart is an abyss of forgiveness, mercy and peace; I love you, child, for hearing Me*, come let us go, discern Me and keep Me company;

26. 1. 87

I, Jesus, love you everlastingly; hear Me and always remember this:

I, Jesus Christ, your Redeemer, love you

* I understood, His Call.

43

from the depths of My Heart; approach Me
and listen to Me; I want you to put
all your trust in Me; have faith in Me;
I want to warn you of what will happen:
having found no evil spirit guiding you,
they will induce in you another theory;
the theory of the subconscious mind
activating you, beloved, which is a
psychological effect of the brain; many
will be gathering against you; many
will be breaking My Law; many will
hound you as a suspect and their wickedness

44

will oppress you; but I will answer for you.
even when I will be proposing peace through
your mouth, they will be all for war;
I am warning you, daughter, let
not your era change you; cling on
Me, your Saviour; I am always near
you; do not let them afflict you,
I will be near you helping you; you
seem sometimes to forget My Presence;
keep Me company; ..... O Vassula, how
I long for the day of glory! .....
why do you keep your question witheld?

45

yes Jesus. The day of glory, what does it mean?

I will tell you: it will be the day when all the revelations will come to light; it will be when all that has been written by Me and My Father will come to light; the Truth will not be concealed; come, now* you are learning;

28. 1. 87

I am here, daughter; I am Wisdom, be ready to deliver My message to all mankind;

*

I understood that the time has not yet come for my mission. I was still learning.

46

I, Jesus Christ, will augment My graces;

(I hesitated here).

Vassula, you are not different in My eyes;

But Jesus, I am different from others, who
received messages from You. Most of them
were religious already. They were nuns who
were devout, but I, I am like the rest
of the world. I do not fit in this picture!

you are thinking in human ways, child;
feel loved by Me;

(Then Jesus, hurrying up, said what
follows. It was as though He wanted
to tell me these things before I opened
my mouth to add more stupidities.)

daughter, come, let us be together, feel

47

loved by Me; come and pray with Me;

(We prayed together.)

glory be to God; free yourself and come closer to Me; lean on Me; delight Me and lean on Me; I want you, Vassula, to understand that I love you; you seem to avoid approaching Me because you feel unfit for Me; you even went as far as to deny Me ...* and instead you asked My servant Daniel to be near you;*²

---

¹ Jesus was really hurt.
*² I felt so unworthy of Jesus that I called my angel Daniel to be with me instead.

48

O daughter, I love you, have I not laid down My life for you?*[1]

It is just that I do not feel worthy of You and Your love!

how could you think this way?*[2] I laid down My life for everyone, worthy and unworthy; leave those thoughts and come to Me; I am calling you so approach Me; allow yourself to rest in Me and never deny Me; I love

*[1] This came out from Him like a long lament.
*[2] Jesus appeared bewildered.

49

you as you are, wretched, helpless and guilty; I have already told you that I will form you; you must leave yourself free in My hands and I will mould you into what I would like you to be; come, beloved, I am with you and I am your Holy Companion guiding you; I, Jesus Christ will reveal you soon, you are to be among mankind;

Jesus You know that I do not understand all what's happening; but my soul rejoices to be with You in this way and my eyes are

50

fixed on You. Now I know that You are a
living Saviour. Here You are, in my room
whispering a message in my ear, chosen out
of thousands to be sent out to the nations
with Your love hymn, what can I ask more?
although many will be confounded by Your
choice, Your Yearnings will win their hearts;
You, who set out from Your Throne, leaving
royal crown aside, You came down again
this very minute to lift my soul from this
exile. O yes, I want to follow You!

I am glad to take you with Me; follow
Me and remember, all that you will be
doing will be done with Me; I will be
your guide, your lamp and your shelter
till the end; then, I, Myself, shall come
and deliver you; call Me when you wish,

51

call Me and I shall descend from heaven;
do not forget My Presence; abandon yourself entirely to Me and I will consume you
with My love; your wretchedness appeals to
Me; come and glorify Me with the love
you have for Me; accept My teachings
for they are meant to feed many;
salvation comes from Me; let Me tell
you: the poor will receive as much as they
want to eat; I am known to never forget
the poor; so come and let Me thrust you
in the depths of My Heart; My love is

52

fathomless; remain in My Heart and you
will be healed, daughter;

29. 1. 87

I am Yahweh your Heavenly Father, Creator
of heaven and earth; daughter, little one,
My dearest, I love you; fulfill My message,
do not fear, I am always beside you;
go and declare My Word and deliver My
message to all mankind; do not fear,
I shall open your mouth in prayer, I
will fill you with the spirit of understanding; you will toil day and night

53

but not in vain; accept My messages, beloved; you will walk with Me; I will be your guide; do not worry for I will supply every want in due time;

(Later on, Jesus spoke.)

it is I, Jesus, come, Vassula; all the messages are given by My Father and Me; fulfill My Words; do not fear; I will remain with you; I will be teaching you; I will be your inheritance; come let us go together;

54

29. 1. 87

follow Me, beloved, I am Jesus Christ;

Am I hurting You Jesus, unwillingly?
I have this tendency to wrong-doing.

you will grieve Me, daughter, were you to
abandon Me; loving Me as you do
rejoices Me; do you not understand? realize
that by leaving Me I will get offended
Vassula; I, Jesus, have taught you
to love Me;

Jesus, what is the proof it is You in all this

look at yourself, you are the proof; you
are the proof of My love;

55

Vassula, I roused you from nothingness to be with Me, so come to your Consoler, approach Me and do not fear Me; I will form you so that you bring back My sons and My daughters from far away; many of those who bear My Name yet have forsaken Me will be adopted by Me as I am adopting you now; so thrust yourself in My Heart; Vassula, every time I feel your heart I find a soft spot on which I can always rest My head; I feel I can rely on you

56

giving Me rest; I, Jesus, love you; remember that your sufferings are Mine too; lean on Me today and offer Me all your love; I need to be comforted;

(I was stunned that Jesus wanted comfort from me.)

How can I comfort You Lord?

by letting Me rest on that soft spot; today I have someone whom I love that will hurt Me once more; fill Me with your consolation ....

What could I do to console You, Lord?

57

let Me leave My Cross on you again; un-
burden Me, let Me rest; I want you to
bear it for Me because I trust you;
O daughter, do not deny Me ever again
like the other day! *

Forgive me. I had felt so unworthy that
I was tempted to call Your servant and
refuse You. I will not do it again.

O daughter, I know, but have I not
laid down My life for all of you? here
now I entrust you with My Cross; soon

---

* I had called my angel and pushed away
Jesus.

58

you will realize how heavy My Cross is; later on I will come back to relieve you; this is the way you and I will work together; we will help each other in this way;

- 30. 1. 87

I want to thank You Father for delivering me from evil. My Saviour, I have never thanked You enough when You came all the way from heaven, to me. All the time You have been my Protector. and Redeemer. When I was surrounded by evil, my soul suffered. When Satan attacked me, with lies and fabrications You did not wait. You came to my rescue. Demons were all around me to kill me, and so my soul, remembering Your works of old, cried out to You.

59

You came to me full of pity, delivering my soul from their clutches. May you be blessed and Your Name glorified.

all Wisdom comes from Me; when I heard your cry in the days of your ordeal I lifted you to My breast; I, Yahweh am your Redeemer; I wanted you, daughter, to need Me; I wanted to remind you of My Mercy; O daughter, your soul had been close to death; all evil was surrounding you,*

---

* This was when I was attacked by Satan, when he realized that God had plans on me; he together with his demons wanted to kill me. God allowed this to happen so that I cry out to Him, need Him and abandon myself to Him.

60

attacking you; they despised you; becoming
their sport they sought to take away
your life and devour you when they
heard of My Plans; among fury ravaging
you I heard from earth your plea; how
could I resist? I could no longer see
you surrounded by evil*, I came rushing
to you enveloping your helpless soul in
My arms, lifting you in My graciousness
to Me; I revived you when My Light

* I was attacked by the demons so viciously
that when I called out to my angel the only
thing he could tell me was: "Pray!" My angel
too was in this battle helping to protect me.

61

shone on you; daughter, I will make you understand fully: I am your God and because you are precious in My eyes I will protect your soul; I am your first Father, have I not told you all about it and revealed it long ago? do not be afraid, daughter, whom I have chosen; I, Yahweh will show My mercy to mankind and I will heal many; I, Yahweh have appointed you to be My bearer well before you were born; you are to bear My message of peace and love and many will learn

62

to live truly a holy life in Me; I will help you glorify Me and I will continue to teach you, daughter; I will heal you from your guilt and I will give you My Peace, from My Heart where I wish you to abide forever; I, Yahweh, will guide you till the end; I love you, never forget this; I am Wisdom and all Wisdom will come from Me;

31. 1. 87

Jesus?

I Am; I am here; I, Jesus Christ am

63

your Teacher, your Spouse and your God;
Vasula, listen to Me carefully now:
My Father has chosen you to be His
bearer; I have come to you in your nothingness and revealed My Heart to you, blessing
you; in all His sovereignty My Father
conveyed you to His servant Daniel* to
attract your attention; during this period,
when he held you fast, to bring you
to Us,*² you were attacked; the devil knowing of My Plans, tried to discourage you,

* My guardian angel.   *² The Holy Trinity

64

in the beginning you had no love for Me; yet I was near you all the time telling you that I love you, but you were cold and indifferent towards Me; afflicted by untimely mourning My Heart ached with sorrow; how was it that Our own child would fall corrupting Our Image to that extent? where had the beauty of Our work gone? so that you see straight again We[1] had to inflict on you the extreme penalty of your rebellion;[2] you sinned

[1] *The Holy Trinity*   [2] *He allowed Satan to attack me.*

65

but you were still Ours; then, in the
middle of your ordeal, I heard your plea,
you were beginning to realize that I, your
Lord, could be your Refuge; to make
you turn to Me and surrender I had to
order you to withdraw from writing;
yes, I shut the doors to heaven; I
whirled you away by My breath of justice; I whirled you away so that you
truly repent; I wanted you to need Me;
I wanted you to love Me ♡ I made
you feel the touch of death, but I made

66

you surrender yourself to Me as you remember;
I had then sent you My angel Daniel
back to you to heal your wounds which
were part of your ordeal; Daniel's work
was to bring you to Us; it was I who
called you; I nursed you back to
health with love and tenderness; I charmed
you with My beauty, I healed you so
that you would be, a fruitful tree;
I showered down learnings and discernment
on you and dictated to you My messages;
I am revealing My Face to you all;

67

Wisdom is delivering her resources not only
to the just but to the unjust too;
I love all of you; so I tell you:

grow in My Spirit, grow like the
cedars spreading your branches wide; I
have raised you to be My bearer to bring
back to Me all those who are leading
wicked and foolish lives; I will take you
on My wings and go around My vault;
covering the earth like mist, from heights
to depths, across the seas I will take you;
and you will cover the whole earth

68

with My message; Vassula, try and perceive what is written; I am your Strength, so do not fear; all the revelations I am giving you will come to light; I am your support and I love you; accept My teachings, I am instructing you to be My follower ♡ instruction comes from Me; Wisdom loves life and shares out her works with the simple; I will give you that ever-flowing River in abundance; then, like a drop of morning dew falling on the ground, I

69

will send you out to all mankind; I will give you to them as My gift, thus enabling them to understand Me more, for <u>this is My Will</u> ♡

O. daughter, how I ♡ long for this day!

Vassula with Her Angel Daniel

Messages of Great Themes

Vassula's Maturing Process

Fr. Michael O'Carroll, C.S.Sp.

The first part of this book showed exactly, through the sequence of relevant messages, how Vassula was initiated, step by step, into the world of the supernatural where she was to find her true vocation. The pages which follow will stimulate the reader's interest in the maturing process through which she passed under the guidance of the Holy Spirit. In the spiritual growth—which was her gift from the Spirit—she was equipped to set forth with clarity and conviction the great themes which are essential to the structure of her concrete and precise teaching: The Two Hearts of Jesus and Mary—implying the intimacy of the Savior with His Mother, the Holy Spirit, Christian Unity, the vital, essential role of East and West, the spiritual resurrection of the Russian Church, the deadly betrayal of the essentials in Church life, the Apostasy and the ensuing purification. Vassula is henceforth open to examination on her accuracy in expounding these salutary truths. For me the result of any such judgment will be favorable. Let each reader form his or her own just conclusion.

The Holy Spirit

*...My Holy Spirit is the Heart of My Body
which is the Church...*

April 15, 1991

Lord, come to us in full force with Your Holy Spirit. For, most tender Abba, as You glorified Your Son and Your Son glorified You, the hour has come that Your Holy Spirit of Truth glorifies Your Son. Prove to the world that Your Word is something alive and active and not just printed words on paper. Let Your Holy Spirit "turn the hearts of fathers towards their children and the hearts of children towards their fathers." Ml 3:24

Peace be with you. Vassula, Scriptures never lie; it has been said that in the last days to come, people will keep up the outward appearance of religion but will have rejected **the inner power** of it *(2 Tm 3:5)*. Ah! my beloved, will there be any faith left on My Return?...

—The inner power of My Church is My Holy Spirit in it, alive and active; like a heart in a body, My Holy Spirit is the Heart of My Body which is the Church.

—The inner power of My Church is My Holy Spirit who gives freely and distributes its gifts and its graces, so that the Church gets some benefit.

—The inner power of My Church is My Holy Spirit, the Reminder of My Word, revealing nothing new, but the same instructions given by the same Spirit.

—The inner power of My Church is My Holy Spirit, that transfigures, uplifts and turns you into real copies of Myself.

—The inner power of My Church is My Holy Spirit, this Fire which enlivens you, purifies you and makes out of your spirit columns of fire; ardent braziers of love, living torches of light, to proclaim without fear My Word, becoming witnesses of the Most High and teaching others to look only for Heavenly things.

—The inner power of My Church is My Holy Spirit, the Life and the Breath that keeps you alive and makes your spirit desire Me,

266

calling Me: Abba. If you refuse, My child, and suppress the gifts of My Holy Spirit, **what services will you be able to do and offer Me?** Do not be like corpses that keep up the outward appearance of religion but reject the inner power of it, with futile speculations; thus limiting Me in My Divinity. Do not stop those who come, as children, to Me, living a life of devotion to the Holy Spirit. It is I, who calls them to the wedding of My Holy Spirit. **The secret of holiness is:** devotion to Me your God, and you can do nothing of yourselves, unless My Spirit living in you guides you and teaches you Heavenly things.

I tell you truly, whoever fears Me will accept My correction. So do not sleep now, for these **are** the Times when one should be awake and vigilant, more than ever. These are the Times to open your ears and listen to My Spirit and not disregard it. Do not play the sage at the wrong moment by pushing the Breath of My Holy Spirit aside and suppressing the inner power that activates My Church. You want to be prudent? Open your eyes then. You want to be prudent? Open your heart and your ears, My friend, not your mind. A prudent person never scorns a warning from the Spirit; only the proud do not know anything about fear. The fear of the Lord is the beginning of Wisdom. You want to be prudent? Look for the Truth that desperately leans over your misery to save you! Look Who is bending towards your wretchedness and your wickedness to pull you to Him and lift you from your graves to breathe Life into you again!

O come! Do not misunderstand Me. **I am not forcing you nor am I trying to violate your liberty!** I have taken pity on your generation; do not say that all I had to say has been said. Why limit Me as yourself?

I am the **Reminder of My Word,** yes, **the inner power of My Church** and I am **free** to send you new portents and do fresh wonders. I am free to raise your generation and pour healing ointment on you from the Riches of My Sacred Heart; when I wish and on whom I wish. I am building, yes, re-building My Church that lies now in ruin; so do not let Me face you, generation, in the Day of Judgment and be obliged to tell you: you were one of My persecutors who pulled down while I used to build. Mercy is at your doors now and My Compassion knocks on your doors in your times of tribulations. You say yourselves holy? Prove yourselves holy by showing Me your adoration; prove yourselves holy by showing Me the souls you are converting and bringing to Me, for My Kingdom consists not in spoken words, nor of **an outward appearance of religion,** but an Inner Power that only I can give you through My Holy Spirit. If you seek it; feel My Presence and My Love I have for each one of you. I, Jesus Christ, am present and bless you all out of the depths of My Sacred Heart, leaving My Sigh of Love on your forehead. Be one; ecclesia shall revive. ΙΧΘΥΣ

Unity

...take My Cross of Unity and carry It
across the world....

October 7, 1991

I want to put everything I have for Your Glory. I do not have much; in fact, I have next to nothing because I am insufficient, poor, weak and most wretched. Yet whatever I might have, take it my Lord.

My closeness (*His intimacy*) to you has lit a fire inside you and saved you and others—I want your free will. Offer yourself to Me and I shall make rivers flow out of you. I need intense poverty to bring My Works out on the surface; I will supply your soul since you are My bride. Vassula, your cities are filled with dead and their stench rises all the way to heaven. They are decomposing by the millions. Pray, pray for peace, love, faith and unity. The Holy One is tormented about that which has to come, saddened beyond description. I will have to let My Hand fall on this evil generation. Daughter, for My sake, take My Cross of Unity and carry It across the world. Go from country to country and tell those who speak of unity, yet never cease to think the contrary and continue to live the contrary, that **their division has separated My Heart from theirs.** Shout and eventually My Voice shall break through their deafness; I am with you in this desolation so do not fear.

I have entrusted you with My Cross. This Cross will sanctify you and save you; and so carry It with love and humility. Invoke My

Name without cease. Your Mission, My child, is to witness for Love and to demonstrate My Holiness in their lack of love and fidelity. Go forward without fear and be My Echo. Witness with joy, with fervor, witness with love for Love. Whenever My enemies pierce you, **rejoice!** And offer all your wounds to Me and I shall soothe you immediately. Every time you lift your eyes looking for Me, My Heart rich in Mercy will not resist you. You are My child whom I adopted, raised and fed; so do not fear men. They cannot destroy you; soon I shall set you free. In the meantime, go around with My Cross of Unity and glorify Me. Be the

defender

of the Truth and of the One Church I Myself had established. Go to every nation and present yourself to them. Tell them that I want Peace and One Church under My Holy Name. Tell them that he who maintains to be just, yet remains divided, will eat from the fruit he has sown and will perish. Tell them also how I abhor insincere hearts; their solemnities and their discourses weary Me. Tell them how I turn away from their loftiness and their rigidity; their judgment appears indeed great and impressive to men but not to Me. I cannot congratulate a dying church nearing putrefaction. Tell those who want to hear that:

> **Unless they lower their voices,**
> **they will never hear Mine.**

Should they lower their voices then they will begin to hear Mine and thus do My Will.

I am One, yet each one of them made a Christ of their own. I am The Head of My Body, yet all I see are their heads, not Mine. Tell them to lower their heads **and they will see Mine.** Tell them to lower themselves so that I may be able to lift them to Me—do not let them terrify you, My child. Be patient as I am patient; be prudent by remaining by My side. You will wear My Jewels (*His Cross, Nails and Thorned Crown*) so that you remain faithful to Me. They will keep reminding you of Me. Pray, My bride. Pray to your Spouse and I shall in the end reward you. Glorify Me and I tell you: toil, sacrifice and nothing will go in vain. Tell everyone that I shall establish My Kingdom in the midst of those very ones who have time to hear My Spirit. Adore Me and do My Will; in these My Soul rejoices! Daughter, I love you in spite of your misery. Allow Me to continue My Works in you; adjust to Me as I adjust to you and through you My Presence will be felt, and in you I shall draw this generation to unity. Be confident because I am with you. My Seal is on your forehead and with this Seal and with My Grace, My Kingdom on earth will be established as I want. Have My Peace. Remember: I am with you all the time. Come, enter into My Wounds. IXΘΥΣ ⟨fish symbol⟩

Unity

...since I Am is One, you too will be one as We are One....

October 14, 1991

Lord?

I Am. Evangelize with love for Love; be rooted in Me, My child. Hand over everything to Me and allow Me to be your Spiritual Director, directing you and giving you My directives for the unification of My Churches. You are to be a sign for them and they will learn that since I Am is One, you too will be one as We are One. Scriptures will be fulfilled because My Sacerdotal Prayer to the Father will be accomplished. I am in you so do not fear. *This is very promising Lord!* Your mission, little one, is to bring My people under one Name, My Name, and break bread together. There is no need to worry. Do your best and I will do the rest. I need humility to accomplish My Works in you and thus bring everything on the surface—your faithless generation, that sheds so much Blood from Me, will rebuff you. But, My Vassula, I shall hold you on your feet in spite of the impressive wounds you will receive from this evil generation. Help will be given to you from above; I have preached to you and to others. Do not stop there. Forward the Teachings I have given you both in public and in your homes. I know how frail you are, but I also know what I have chosen.

Lord I feel content to know that we will be united, although no one yet really knows how. The problems are apparently great and the schisms greater still. As you say: "The staff of the Shepherd has been broken not only in half, but in splinters. And Your Body has been mutilated, wrenched and paralysed." You ask us all to bend. How? What is to be done? Which is the first step?

I am a Greek Orthodox and I am sharing with my Roman Catholic brothers everything, and I do not differentiate myself under Your Name when I am with them; nor do they treat me any differently from their own.

I also know that many of them go to the Greek or Russian Orthodox churches...

Speak up, child!

Give me the right words Lord.

Say:...and they are not allowed to share Your Body.

No. They are not allowed, although our Sacraments are the same. Yet we, Orthodox are allowed to share Your Body; I was even told I was ex-communicated because I go to the R. Catholics not to say more. I am also persecuted from both sides because my confessor is a R. Catholic! And You do witness all this my Lord Jesus!

Yet, the day will come when they will break bread together on one altar. And no one will stop My children coming to Me. No one will ask them: "Are you an Orthodox?"[1] This fortress they have built to divide you is already condemned by Me; you are all brothers in Me. This is what you are to teach them to believe and persuade them to do—as for those who remain divided in body and spirit differentiating themselves under My Holy Name, I tell them, as I have told the church in Sardis *(Ap 3)*: you are reputed to be alive in the eyes of the world, but not in your Maker's Eyes. Revive what little you have left: it is dying fast and wherever the corpse is, there will the vultures gather. Unite! Assemble! Invoke My Name together! Consecrate My Body and My Blood together! Do not persecute the Way! Humble yourselves and bend to be able to unite and glorify Me. You speak of the Spirit but do not act in the Spirit. You speak of the Way but

1. Apparently the Greek and Russian Orthodox priests have the right to ask the person who wants to receive Holy Communion whether they 'belong' to them. They refuse the R. Catholics from receiving Holy Communion, although the Sacraments are the same.

you rank first to obstruct It!—How little do you know Me... You call out My Name, yet you murder My children between the sanctuary and the altar. I tell you solemnly, all of this will be brought to you in the Day of Judgment. Can you face Me and truly say: "I am reconciled with My brothers." Can you truly say: "I have not differentiated myself among brothers. Under Your Holy Name; I have treated them as my equal." When you present your case before Me I shall then say to your face:

"Away with you, you have not treated your brothers as your equal; you have massacred daily My Body. Where is your triumph? While I was building, you were tearing down. **While I was reassembling you were scattering.** While I was uniting you were dividing!"

Yet, even today, if you come to Me as you are, I can heal you. I can transfigure you and you will glorify Me. "Alas for those with child, or with babies at the breast when My Day comes!" Write:[1] Alas for those I find with sin coiled in them as with child and with adepts formed by them and of their own kind. But it has been said that from your own ranks there will be men coming forward with a travesty of the truth on their lips to induce the disciples to follow them (Acts 20:30). I am shouting and I am trying to break through your deafness to save you, and if I reproach you it is because of the

Greatness of the Love
I have for you.

But I tell you truly: I shall assemble one day **all** the separated parts of My Body together into One assembly—do not weep My friend[2] You who love Me, endure what I endure; however, console Me and have faith in Me. You will achieve great works in My Name; be tolerant as I am tolerant. I had been hungry, thirsty and often starving and you came to My help. Carry on your good works and I shall reward you. I tell you truly, you are not alone; I am with you. Be united in Me and live in peace; you are the posterity of My Blood and the heir of My Kingdom. Tell them that the Heart of the Lord is Love and that the Heart of the Law is based on Love. Tell My people

---

1. Jesus means the explanation of this verse of Lk 21:23.
2. Jesus speaks to those who truly love Him and are truly and sincerely working to unite the Churches, His friends.

that I do not want administrators in My House. They will not be justified in My Day because it is these very ones who have industrialized My House. I have sent you My Spirit to live in your hearts. This is why the Spirit that lives in you will show you that My Church will be rebuilt inside your hearts and you will acknowledge each other as your brother in your heart. *(My Jesus, in saying all this, had taken the voice of a victim. Weary, begging, as though He depended on us—like a prisoner in a cell going to the door of his cell and asking the guard, from the little window, how much longer yet was his sentence, before the day of his liberation.)*

Will I, brother, one more season go through the pain I have been going through year after year? Or will you give Me rest this time? Am I going to drink one more season the Cup of your division? Or will you rest My Body and unify, for My sake, the Feast of Easter?

In unifying the date of Easter, you will alleviate My pain, brother, and you will rejoice in Me and I in you. And I will have the sight of many restored; "My Beloved! My Creator! He who is my husband has revealed to us things that no human hand could have performed!"

This is what you will cry out, once your sight is restored, in My Name.

—And I will come to you *(Jesus said this as a King, majestically.)—*

I solemnly tell you: summon, assemble all of you, and listen this time to your Shepherd:

I will lead you in the way that
you must go.

Send My Message to the ends of the earth. Courage, daughter, smile when I smile; I am with you to guide your steps to heaven.

ΙΧΘΥΣ

Our Two Hearts

...you have not listened to Our Two Hearts, the Immaculate Heart of My Mother and My Sacred Heart...You have not under-

273

stood. Our Hearts, like Two Olive Trees, one to the right and one to the left, were for so many years trying to revive you....

December 24, 1991 Christmas Eve

My Lord?

I Am. Lean on Me, child.

(I saw with the eyes of my soul Jesus' holy Face. He looked like a child with big innocent eyes.)

Tremendous reparations have to be done to cicatrize the wounds of this earth; wounds and cuts made by wickedness and sin. Delight the Eyes of your Saviour and expand;

Let it be

that My Message becomes so ample, so vast, testifying itself, that Wickedness, Apathy and Atheism will be seized and will repent. Child! Cling to the hem of My clothes and stretch,[1] even more now, from one corner of the earth to the other. Enter into My Sanctuaries if they welcome you into My Sanctuaries; if men forbid you, do not let this afflict you nor bring you sorrow. Do not despair. Your oppressors will look back in those scenes in the day of the Purification and will weep, remembering their rejection. They will realize how they were rejecting Our Divine Hearts, not you; Our Two Hearts that prophesied. Daughter, follow My blood-stained Footprints and pronounce My Holy Name in any gathering. **The time has come that you should not hesitate anymore.** Plant Vineyards everywhere and anywhere you can. Make gardens out of deserts. I have blessed My Messages to prosper and take root. So, courage, daughter.

(Suddenly I felt a 'sword of fire' pierce me, and I cried out: Lord! I miss You!)

You miss Me because you saw My Glory.... Write: citadel after citadel is being besieged by the Rebel; I come today and offer all mankind My Peace but very few listen. Today I come with peace-terms and a Message of Love, but the peace I am offering is blas-

---

1. Jesus means to widen the scope, in spreading His urgent message.

phemed by the earth and the Love I am giving them is mocked and jeered in this Eve of My Birth. Mankind is celebrating these days without My Holy Name. My Holy Name has been abolished and they take the day of My Birth as a great holiday of leisure, worshipping idols. Satan has entered into the hearts of My children, finding them weak and asleep. I have warned the world. Fatima's Message speaks: that in My Day I shall make the sun go down at noon and darken the earth in broad daylight. I will allow the Dragon to bite this sinful generation and hurl a Fire the world has never seen before nor will ever come to see again, to burn her innumerable crimes. You will ask: "Will all the inhabitants perish, the good with the bad?"

I tell you: the living will envy the dead; out of two men one will be taken. Some will ask: "Where are Elijah and Moses who are to come?" I tell you, you evil generation: We[1] have not been speaking in parables all these years. Elijah and Moses have come already and you have not recognized them but treated them as you pleased. You have not listened to Our Two Hearts, the Immaculate Heart of My Mother and My Sacred Heart. You faithless generation...Our Two Hearts have not been speaking to you in parables nor in riddles. All Our Words were Light and Our Hearts, like Two Lamps, are shining near each other so bright that everyone may see.

But, you have not understood. Our Hearts, like Two Olive Trees (*Ap 11:4 & Zc 4:3*), one to the right and one to the left, were for so many years trying to revive you. Like Two Olive Branches pouring oil (*Zc 4:12*) to heal your sick generation and cicatrize your wounds, but your generation treated Our Two Hearts as they pleased. Our Two Hearts are anointed (*Zc 4:14*) and are living.

They are like a sharp sword, double-edged (*Ap 1:16*), prophesying. But the rebellious spirit in this generation is recrucifying My Word (*Allusion to Ap 11:8-10*) the double-edged sword, and are rejecting Our Two Hearts who speak to you today. Just like Sodom's and Egypt's rejection of My messengers, this era's stubbornness has surpassed Pharaoh's, because their claims to their knowledge have become a battlefield to My Knowledge (*Allusion to Ap 11:7*).

---

1. Christ means the Two Hearts who are the two witnesses in Ap 11:1-13 and in Zc 4:1-14

Indeed Our Two Hearts have become a plague to the people of the world *(Ap 11:10)*, but soon, very soon now, My Voice shall be heard again. I shall visit you by thunder and fire. Justice is at hand; and Our Two Hearts you have combated shall prevail in the end *(Allusion to Ap 11:11)*; and the kingdom of the world will become My Kingdom *(Ap 11:15)*. This is all very close now; open your eyes and look around you. I am giving you all the signs of the Times; and you, you who are laboring to bring to the surface the devotion of the Alliance of the Two Hearts, do not lose courage.

The Book of Apocalypse speaks as well as the Book of Zechariah of this Truth. Do not fear. Spread this devotion with trust and with courage.

My Holy Spirit

...happy the man who opens his heart to My Holy Spirit. He will be like a tree along a river, yielding new fruit every season...

October 5, 1992

Father, once, before Your Majesty revived the memory of my poor soul, I had forgotten who had made me. The next moment You restored my memory. You asked me to lift up my eyes to the heavens, then a ray of Light shone on me and like a consuming fire, Your Spirit rested on me. True Light, Inexhaustible Treasure, You are awe-inspiring, and Stupendously Great! How can I not thank and praise You, most Tender Father for resting Your Spirit on my wretched soul and making Your Spirit one with me?

Peace be with you. It is I, Yahweh, your Eternal Father, the One who taught you with Wisdom. I am the Holy One who approached you in your misery and healed you; I spoke to you in your sleep and from thereon the scales of your eyes having dropped, you have seen the Light. I have taught you, daughter, not to fear Me, but to fear Me only when you reject Me and rebel against Me. I have taught you to dwell in confidence in My Presence showing you My Infinite Tenderness and the Fatherly Love I have for each one of you. I Myself have plucked your sins by the roots and in their place with the space given Me. I planted My graces in you; although your soul leaped like

276

on fire, I had to continue My route in your soul and overthrow all the rivals who kept house with you. In My Jealous Love I replaced those rivals with abundant fruit and henceforth I became your table-companion, your delight! Listen now, My daughter, My Own, write and tell My children this:

From the depths of My Heart I call to you all! Blessed are the ones who have ears to hear. If it were not for My prophets, can you then name Me who foretold the coming of My Son? If you say you live by the Truth and in My Love, how is it then that your generation today cuts out My prophets and persecutes them just as your ancestors used to do? Out of My Infinite Mercy a City is being rebuilt for My Own people. Will this City renewed be rebuilt on the blood of those you will eternally persecute? Today more than ever I am sending you My Holy Spirit to renew you. Yet for how long will this generation keep resisting My Holy Spirit? Tell Me, can a body live without a heart? Learn that My Holy Spirit is the Heart of the Body which is the Church; learn that My Holy Spirit is the Breath of the Church, the Essence of zeal for Me your God. My Holy Spirit is the sweet Manna of Heaven nourishing the poor. Happy the man who opens his heart to My Holy Spirit; he will be like a tree along a river, yielding new fruit every season, with leaves that never wither but are medicinal. Happy the man who opens his heart to My Holy Spirit, like a crystal clear stream. My Spirit shall flow like a river in his heart, renewing him. For wherever this river flows, life springs up, and joy! Have you not read:

The River of Life, rising from My Throne and from the Lamb will flow down in the middle of the city street? My Holy Spirit will shy away from malicious souls, but will show Himself openly to the innocent, to the poor and to the simple. With great joy My Holy Spirit will envelop these souls and become their Holy Companion and their Guide, and as they walk, their going will be unhindered. As they run, they will not stumble, and should they drink deadly poison they will remain unharmed. Should they meet a legion of demons on their route, they will go by unscathed. My Holy Spirit will teach them the sweetness that exhales from Me, the depths of My Eternal Love. My Holy Spirit will take the innocent and make a pact of Love and Peace with them, to become fit and become His partner. My Holy Spirit will lift them and carry them, like a bridegroom carrying his bride across the threshold. He too will carry them behind the walls of the sanctuary where lie fathomless riches and mysteries, mysteries that no eye has seen before. And like a Spouse adorning His Bride with jewels He too will adorn them with imperial knowledge to delight in throne and scepter. O what will My Holy Spirit not do for you!

My Holy Spirit is the zest of your life, the Royal Crown of Splendor, the Diadem of Beauty from My Mouth, the radiant Glory of the Living One, the Secret Revelation of your creation. My Holy Spirit is the flavor of your homelies in My Assemblies and the fulfillment of your Times....He is the Flaming Fire of your heart and the perception of My Mysteries. My Holy Spirit is the theme of your praises to Me revealing to your heart that I Am Who I Am, revealing to your spirit that I am your

Abba,

and that you **are** My offspring. My seed...blessed be the pure in heart: they shall see Me. Rejoice and be glad and open up to receive My Holy Spirit so that you too may delight and hear My Voice! Open your hearts and you shall see My Glory, and like a child needing comfort My Holy Spirit will comfort you, whose love for you surpasses any human love.

I, the Creator of the heavens and earth tell you, My Holy Spirit is the Spouse of the Bride, of She who held the Infant Who was to save you and redeem you, and in Whom through His Blood you would gain freedom and forgiveness of your sins. He is the Spouse of the One Whom He found like a garden enclosed, holding the rarest essences of virtues, a sealed fountain, the loveliest of Women, bathed in purity because of Her unique perfection. My Spirit came upon Her and covered Her with His shadow and glorified Me making Her the Mother of God, the Mother of all humanity and the Queen of Heaven.[1] Such is the Richness of My Holy Spirit....I am showering on all of you My Holy Spirit, now...today....I, Yahweh, the Almighty am telling you:

---

1. I want to note that when the Father was dictating to me this passage concerning Our Blessed Mother, if He were not God, I would have said He was exalted, so much was His Joy.

278

I am giving you all this free gift to save you out of the greatness of the Love I have for you. Love and Loyalty now descend. I Yahweh lean down from heaven to embrace all of you, My saving help is offered from above to you; are you willing to comply with My given Law? Are you willing to entrust Me with your soul? Do not say I am unmoved by your misery and unresponsive to your prayers. If the flames lick up your countries and fires devour your people and if the inhabitants of the earth taste the disgrace of death it is all due to your great apostasy. You have shunned from My Holy Spirit, He who would have clothed you in blessings, He who would have made your heart and flesh leap and sing for joy to Me your God. But you preferred to become homeless, beggared and fatherless and today dwindling away in the shadows of death. How I pity you....O generation! How much longer can you defy Me?

My Love fills the earth. My calls fill the mouths of My envoys and though My grief is acute and My Justice is now brimming over. I can still relent and I can accept the homage you would offer Me. I am ready to forgive you through the Blood shed by My Son and through His Sacrifice if you take My Words to heart. Soon, very soon now, My Holy Spirit will blow on you with such force, making a mighty sound ring out at the four corners of the earth, as a reminder before all the inhabitants of the earth. Then immediately at the sound of My Holy Spirit's Breath, the people of the earth all together would fall on their face to the Ground in adoration of Me the Lord, the Almighty, the Most High, and in the end the people would bow low before the Throne of the Lamb and receive the Blessing from the Throne. And now, I who created you and I who formed you, ask you: will I deign to hear your cry of repentance?

A Warning

...Have they understood the words: reconciliation, peace, love and unity? When brimstone and devouring flames will take place—and they are very near you now—they will learn that I had sent a prophet among them;...

December 13, 1992

Our Father, who art in Heaven, hallowed be thy Name....Our Father, whose love is revealed to the least of us, have mercy on Your creation! You have given us as a free gift: our liberty, to use as we please, but we have turned our liberty against us. Like a razor-blade in an infant's hand, we use it, hacking ourselves to death...O come! and turn our attention to Your Holy Name, or we will slice ourselves to pieces! I invoke you God Almighty in our troubles, will You rescue us, or will you hide from my petition?

Daughter, you are in charge of My Message, and I have been sending you in the world from nation to nation to cry out repentance and reduce this wilderness. Indeed, the crowds throng around you. It has come to their ear that I Am is speaking, and nation after nation is talking about you. They say to each other: "Let us go and hear what God is saying." They come in thousands and sit down in front of you and listen to your words but who acts on them? As far as they are concerned, you are like a love song beautifully sung to music. Your words enchant them. But, who among them puts My Messages into practice? Have they understood the words: reconciliation, peace, love and unity? When brimstone and devouring flames will take place—and they are very near you now—they will learn that I had sent a prophet among them. From the beginning I had given you My Commandments; I had asked you to love Me, your Lord, with all your heart, with all your soul, and with all your mind. Today I am asking you to allow Me to touch your soul so that your heart will be able to praise Me and tell Me that neither death nor life, no angel, no prince, nothing that exists, nothing still to come, not any power, or height or depth, nor any created thing, will ever come between you and your love to Me. I am your Stronghold; know that My Love is revealed even to the very least of you. Do not search your salvation in the light of the world, since you know that the world cannot give you Life. Soon My Throne and that of the Lamb will be in its place and your soul will be renewed with My Transcendent Light; because I, your Father, intend to restore the memory of your soul and make your heart sing to Me the word Abba—Father!

I tell you, you do not belong to the world, so why do you still allow yourselves to be deceived over and over again?—Since the foundations of the earth I have called you by your name, but, when I proposed Peace, universal Peace, nearly all of you were for war. Yet, I am pouring out My Holy Spirit now to remind you of your true foundations and that all of you are My seed; but today My seed is filled up with dead words....I am the Holy One who held you first; for how long will your soul resist Those Eyes who saw you first? And for how long will your soul deny My distressed calls? Many of you are still fondling the Abomination of the Desolation in the most profound domain of your soul. Can you not see how the Viper repeatedly is deceiving you in the same way he deceived Adam and Eve?

Satan is suggesting to you, untiringly and subtly to cut off all your heavenly bonds that bond you to Me, **your Father in heaven**. He mesmerized the memory of your soul to make you believe you are fatherless, thus creating a gulf between you and Me, your God. Satan wants to separate you from Me and cut off your umbilical cord that unites you to Me in which Rivers of Life flow into you.

Generation, you have still not set your minds for Me. When will you decide to return to Me? Do you want to pass this era's threshold by blazing fire, by brimstone and devouring flame? How could your soul trade My Glory for a worthless imitation that the evil one offers you daily? Ask Me for **your daily bread** and I shall give it to you! Why are you all so willing to listen to the Viper? You and I know that Satan is the father of lies, then why are you still listening to him?

I, your Creator, am your Father and I am calling you back to Me. Believe in My distressed calls. Will your soul continue to befriend the Rebel, or will you deign to come down from your throne and repent? It is for you to decide—there is not much time left. I am reminding you to beware of the false teachers and the false prophets who induce in your soul desolation and misinterpret the gospels, telling you that the Holy Spirit is not with you to remind you of your foundations, nor of where you come from. They have already made a desolation out of your soul and dug a vast gulf between you and Me your Father. Do not let them expand this desolation in your soul and mislead you into believing I have left you orphans. These false prophets have made out of My Son, Jesus, a liar and out of the gospels an echoing cymbal, empty with emptiness. They made out of My Word a gaping grave.

So beware of those false teachers, who tell you that My Holy Spirit cannot descend to perform in you miracles and wonders. Beware of them who condemn My Holy Spirit who, in your days more than anytime, reminds you of your foundations. Beware of them who keep up the outward appearance of religion but reject the inner power of it; the inner power that is My Holy Spirit. And, if anyone of you is calumniated and dejected because you are witnessing the Truth, turn to your Holy Mother; She will console your soul and provide you with courage.

If the world inflicts on you impressive wounds, turn to your Mother and she will dress your wounds with her Maternal Love and Affection; like She took care of My Beloved Son, your Holy Mother will take care of you too. In your misery and distress She comes flying to you and takes you into Her Heart; that same Heart who conceived your Saviour. Your Holy Mother in Heaven will teach you to enlarge My Kingdom on earth by teaching you to love Me.

So let love be the principle of your life; let love be your root. Allow Me, your Father, to bond you to Me; allow Me to touch your soul. Come to Me and thrust yourself into My Arms; what greater bliss than being held by those Hands that created you? Place your ear on My Mouth, this Mouth that breathed in you through your nostrils: **Life**. And, from the dust of the soil I revived you to conquer the earth. I touched you and asked you to listen to My Word since then; come, you must set your heart right, renounce the iniquities that stain your soul and with all your heart

HALLOW MY NAME

α𝖷Ω

Rebellion

..."*rebellion is at its work already, but in secret, and the one who is holding it back has first to be removed, before the Rebel appears openly;...*

March 17, 1993

Peace be with you. My child, you are to teach My children all that I have given you. Do not fear for I am in front of you and I am your

Shield. No one will ever, no matter how much the evil one tries, come between you and Me. Although Satan mobilizes men to handicap you, and although he makes them join forces against you, never fear. I am the Almighty and My Eyes witness the injustice done to you.

Beloved, I will imbue you with My Strength and I will give to all My children bread in abundance. I will make your zeal for My House devour My enemies. I will make you a threat to them; so never fear, since I Am is standing in front of you. My blessings are upon you and every fibre of your heart will be covered by Courage, Strength and Peace. In this way you will atone for the salvation of souls and for the renewal of My House in the most perfect way.

Lift your voice without fear and prophesy; prophesy, My child, to blot out wickedness from so many hearts! Let those who have ears let them listen to what the Spirit today is saying to the Churches. Let all who are thirsty come. Write and tell My sacerdotal souls this: "Rebellion is at its work already, but in secret, and the one who is holding it back has first **to be removed**, before the Rebel appears openly" (2 Th 2:7).

I tell you, love My Church as I love Her and as I sacrificed Myself for My Church to make Her entirely holy. You too, My priests, sacrifice yourselves to Her, imitate Me. I am telling you all this and I know that My sheep who belong to Me will listen to My Voice and will never fail Me. I am addressing you today to tell you from the core of My Heart the same embittered words I uttered at My Last Supper around My disciples: "someone who shares My table rebels against Me. I tell you this now, before it happens, so that when it does happen you may believe that I am He speaking, today."

My little children, do not let your hearts be troubled, trust in Me, and do not fear. Soon a Baptism of Fire will be sent by the Father to burn the crimes of this world. The hour will come when men of power will enter My Sanctuary; men who do not come from Me. In fact this hour is already here. I, Jesus Christ, wish to warn My priests, bishops and cardinals; I wish to warn all My House of a great tribulation. My Church is approaching a great tribulation. Remember, I have chosen you, by My sanctifying Spirit, to glorify Me. I have chosen you from the beginning to be the sturdy pillars of My Church

283

and to live by faith in the Truth. I have chosen you to share My Glory and to shepherd My lambs.

I tell you solemnly that you will soon be tested by fire; pray and fast so as not to be put to the test. Stand firm and **keep the traditions you were taught. Obey My pope (*John Paul II*) no matter what comes up.** Remain faithful to him and I will give you the graces and the strength you will need. I urge you to **keep faithful to him** and keep away from anyone who rebels against him. Above all, **never listen to anyone who dispels him**; never let your love for him grow insincere. Soon you will be faced with an ordeal as you have never experienced before. My enemies will try to buy you for themselves with insidious speeches. The evil one is at his work already and Destruction is not far away from you. The pope (*John Paul II*) will have much to suffer. This is why you will all be persecuted for proclaiming the Truth and for being obedient to My pope. This is also why they will hate you, because their deeds are evil and indeed, everybody who works for evil hates the Light and avoids it, for fear his actions of Destructiveness should be exposed. I tell you solemnly, every fibre of My Heart is lacerated. If anyone comes your way bringing a different doctrine than the one I Myself instituted, do not listen to him; these people come from the Deceiver. I have laid down My foundation on Peter, the rock....and the gates of the underworld can never hold out against it.... If anyone comes your way and tells you: "Move from your fidelity you have for this pope to another's sound movement," do not move! Beware!

The yeast of the Deceiver may be powerful and might taste good, but in reality it is of **deadly deception!** Do not allow anyone to deceive you; resist the devil's tactics. For today, My priests, you will have to conquer evil with the strength you receive from Me who am the Truth. You will be in a spiritual war as never before with an army which originates from the powers of Darkness. Pray, My beloved ones, all the time. I Am is with you; I love you all; a man could have had no greater love than to have laid down his life for his friends, as I have. You are My friends. Be sincere with one another, love one another and stand firm without fear when the great Tribulation, that now hovers like a black cloud over My House will soon cover it like a black veil. I have told you all this now before it happens, so that when it happens you may believe. ΙΧΘΥΣ

284

Rebellion and Traditions

...one of them living under My roof is betraying Me;...

...they rip My Traditions to install frills and human doctrines;...

...tell them that the God they have forgotten has never forgotten them;...

May 27, 1993

Peace be with you. I am the Alpha and the Omega; remain in Me so that you proclaim My Message as clearly as you ought to; let My Word go out, let every one hear My Call and understand how much I love them; let them know that My Five Wounds are wide open; men have an infinite capacity for treachery and for striking Me....I must tell you with pain and sorrow in My Heart all that I see in My Own House: today the Tyrant is trampling already on My Body and wishes to abolish entirely My Perpetual Sacrifice; one of them living under My roof is betraying Me; He proclaims peace but seeks only evil; he burns incense but it is to summon Satan to gain more power;

Oh Lord! I can hardly believe this is happening...

yet it is happening, you do not seem to understand....he together with his followers are determined to place themselves in My Throne and rule the world in prophet's garments and ah!....so many of My shepherds are led astray with their false teachings and errors; they are leaving the right path and wander to follow a tradition that does not come from Me; they abandon the holy rules that I have given them; I have warned you of these false teachers and false prophets, I have warned you, that in the last days, Babylon will be erected into the heart of My Sanctuary, turning My Holy Place into a den of thieves, into a **haunt of devils!** O daughter!....a lodge for every foul spirit to abide and reign....

They are busy trading in My Own House; these traders are promoting their own in My House, while ensnaring the lives of My people. They are after My prophets. They kill My mouth pieces and spare their own false prophets who expand heresies and errors! They dishonor My prophets in front of the world, lying to the world who love to listen to calumny and insult. They rip My Traditions to install frills and human doctrines; all these things they do in front of My Throne.... These traders are deceiving many with specious arguments. They place their own in the best seats to reign with a scepter of Falsehood.

I have appointed you to be My Echo, so go and proclaim what you have heard. Tell them that you are all living under the Great Apostasy foretold. Tell My shepherds to open their eyes and ears to My anguished calls; for soon they will be forced to eat and drink venom. Summon your communities and prepare them for vigils of prayer and fasting. Satan is on his way to put every one on trial. He is coming to scatter you all and divide you. He is on his way to My Throne in My Tabernacle to sell My Blood and remove My Perpetual Sacrifice *(Jesus was in such pain that He wept.)*

My people...My heritage...to you I cry out. Priests and ministers of My Altar, you who lift Me every day, never give Me up, never sell Me *(More tears from Jesus)*. The wails of the angels are heard already and the heavens tremble with what they see coming. Even the demons are appalled and grow pale....The Enemy, the one who claims to be so much greater than anything that is worshipped will enthrone himself in My Sanctuary. He is on his way, with a noose in his hands, heading for the one who is appointed by Me *(The Pope: John Paul II)*, and who holds the rebellion back from bursting out. Discreet and courageous he is, and his life is being poured out as a sacrifice *(The Pope)*.... I bless him for having a firm grasp of the unchanging Message of the Tradition; but Satan wants to silence him; to be able to expand through the mouths of those who sell My Blood, his *(Satan's)* errors and bring all of you to your ruin. This is Satan's hour; with vile motives of destructing My creation. Cry out, daughter, for that day is near, and it is coming to devastate nation after nation. My Heart is broken.... Love was not afraid to die. So you too My friends and My shepherds; do not fear; follow Me. Your duty is to defend My Word and My Church to death.

Do not say, "let me go first and salute My own." I tell you: "once the hand is upon the shepherd's staff, no one who looks back is worthy of Me or fit for My Kingdom." Follow Me in My Blood-stained Footprints all the way to Calvary. Daughter, My blessed one, your Comforter is pleased that you comforted Him and that you allowed Him to use your hand. Ah....Vassiliki, these Tears of Blood I shed every day are caused by iniquity and wickedness....(*A few moments silence, then again very sorrowfully the Lord cried out.*)...Era! O era! why have you abandoned your God?

(*Here, Christ turned to me and said:*)

My angel, formed by Me, wound Me not but do not leave My Hand now. Some will stone you, some will drag you in mud, some will raise their fists and menace you, but do not fear them. You say that they heap insult upon insult on your head, calumny upon calumny. I tell you, they are only heaping reward upon reward here in heaven for you, and blessing upon blessing on your forehead from Me. So declare without fear My Message. Witness My angel and I shall not pass sentence on many souls on account of the wounds you receive. I will give you a fair wage for the wounds you receive in the House of My friends. I have selected you to be the victim of My Passion, the altar upon which I will lay Unity, so what more could you ask? What more could I give you that I have not yet given you? Wisdom has been given to you and My Spirit is with you to make you endure the scourge of the world and ah...I have given you the gift to thirst for Me and to long for Me, a priceless gift. Therefore, walk with Me and allow Me to use you and send you from nation to nation to tell them that **the God they have forgotten has never forgotten them.** Remind them that the heart of the Lord is Mercy. Yes, tell them that I am gentle and humble of Heart. Jesus is My Name. ic (Greek abbreviation for Jesus Christ).

The Seventh Seal

...I will break the seventh seal and upon this, there will be an awed silence...

...suddenly this silence will be broken with the coming of My Day,...

...Soul, My reign will begin in your days...

June 3, 1993

Lord?

I Am. Unload your burden onto Me, My child....

My ears are getting sick at the howling of the wicked, their malicious tongue is inventing lie upon lie about me.

Your false accusers will have to face Me one day....I am on your side, have you not noticed? All their accusations will drain away like water running to waste! **Rise!** rise and lay your hands on the sick and I will heal them. **Speak!** and the utterance of My Words in your mouth will make their spirit fall in My embrace;[1] Lean on Me, I have given you My Peace, so abide in this Peace. Do not fear now....behold

I am the Resurrection

but the prince of this world is Death. Accuse not your persecutors so that I will not judge you, too, in the Day of Judgment. Soul-of-My-Passion, I, the Lord, am showing you the steps I have taken for My Passion. Since you are serving Me, you must follow Me. What do you want Me to say: "follow Me but not in My Footprints?" This cannot be, whoever serves Me will follow My Blood-stained Footprints.... It is through My Finger that you raise the dead; *(spiritually; conversions)*. Those who **still** do not see My wonders are those that My Kingdom has overtaken *(passed them by)*. My friend, My little friend, look how much Celestial Manna I have been feeding you with; and I, your God, will keep on nourishing you. **No man will push away My Hand from your mouth.** I will be your Strength to fulfill My Plan through your frailty; I am preparing you all for My Kingdom. Write:

The world today rejects Our Two Hearts, the Heart of your Holy Mother and My Sacred Heart. The times you are living in now are times of Mercy. I have already explained to you *(look at message 18.2.93)* what will follow when the sixth seal will be broken. And now hear Me and write:

Just after Our Two Hearts have accomplished the witnessing,[2] I will break the seventh seal and upon this, there will be an awed silence *(Ap 8:1)*....In this silence the people of the world would think they triumphed over Our Two Hearts, and they will rejoice (Ap 11:10) and celebrate the event, because they would believe they got

---

1. Slain in the Spirit—It happened several times in meetings.
2. I believe it means when the time is ready for the Day of the Lord. Ap 11:7.

rid of Our Two Hearts witnessing through Our mouthpieces. Since what they witnessed had become a plague in their ears and a plague to their interests and their evil intentions. Then, suddenly this silence will be broken with the coming of My Day, and woe to the unclean! Woe to the unrepentant. Their corpses will litter this desert, this desert they themselves laid out. My angel then will fill the censer he has been holding in front of My Throne and the altar, with Fire, which he will throw down on to the earth; *(Ap 8:5)* and while everybody will be watching, a violent earthquake will come, and the elements of the earth will catch fire and fall apart *(2 P 3:12)*. Many will take to the mountains to hide in caves *(Ap 6:15)* and among the rocks. They would call out to Me but I will not listen. They will provoke Me and blaspheme My Holy Name and say to the (Ap 6:16) mountains and rocks: 'fall on us and hide us away from the One who sits on the Throne and from the anger of the Lamb', for My Day will come and who can survive it? And the survivors *(Ap 11:13)* will fall on their knees, overcome with fear and will only praise Me their God....Then, the New Heavens and the New Earth *(Ap 21:1)* will come upon you, the kingdom *(Ap 11:15)* of the world will become My Kingdom and I will reign in every heart. The world *(Ap 21:4)* of the past will be gone. Soul, My reign will begin in your days.

A Song to the Lord

...I do not know how to sing, Lord...

...then let Me, together with you, write down the words of a song;...

November 11, 1993

Peace be with you. This is your Lord speaking and it is for My Glory that I am revealing Myself to you[1] and to your society! Come, come and sing a song to Me.

I do not know how to sing, Lord.

You do not know how to sing? Then let Me, together with you,

---

1. Many times the Lord effaces me and shows Himself to people, in my place.

write down the words of a song; then even if you read them out with your heart, their intonation will turn into a melody in My Ears. Write:

Emmanuel come, come My Beloved, come and revive my soul. Come and endow my soul with life!

Oh Beloved of the Father, I have opened the door of my heart. Will I have to wait very long before You step in my chambers? Your mere passage in my heart will leave behind a trail of the most delicate fragrance of Your perfume, because Your Love will remedy my pitiable soul. Spirit of Love, grant me only my share of Your Love. Emmanuel come, come my Perfect One, come and ravish my soul, or else destitution shall overtake my miserable heart!

Oh Beloved of the Father, how Beautiful You are! Son of the Most High, who is like unto You? Come and draw me in Your Footprints. We shall take the road together, we shall follow the signs laid down by Your Father's Hand, leading to His Garden of Delights. We shall, my Beloved, with one single heart and one single mind follow the sweetly-scented trail Your Father laid out for me. To encourage me, He has covered my path with sapphires; He has for my reassurance signed His Holy Name with oil all over me.

Oh Beloved of the Father, You, whose hands are still dripping with pure Myrrh since Your Resurrection, come and ravish my soul with a single one of Your glances: enough for me to keep my soul tranquil and quiet; enough for me to rejoice my eyes in Your Presence. Breath of my garden, Fountain of my soul, Source of Sublime Love, altogether adorable and Holy, of which all fruitfulness comes from You, pour out Your Spirit on all mankind. Display Your Great Love in Heaven and on earth.

Oh Beloved of the Father, You are wholly Beautiful. To what shall I compare You, my Life? To a column of incense smoke, to a ray of glittering Light, to a breath of pure myrrh? Your Presence, Lord, stands majestically before me, and ah, as though I were queen myself, You raise me to embrace my soul, delicately whispering Your Love in my ear:

"My dove, I am sick with love for you. I come from the highest heaven to visit you. I have laid aside My Crown and descended from My Throne. I will not delay, only a little while now, a very little while, and the ban will be lifted. I will renew you and I will give you back your divinity. My beloved, I will give water from the well of Life free to you who thirst for My Love. Your King will take no rest, none at all, beloved of My Soul; not until you allow Him to seal on your heart His Divine Kiss; a Kiss from His Mouth. *(S.s. 1:1)* Have you not noticed how the sun darkens every time you doubt of My Love?

Approach Me dearest soul, and I will pour out on you countless treasures from My Sacred Heart. For you alone I have stored them, to turn your soul fair as in springtime and into an ivory tower; a Heaven for Myself alone. Have you not realized how I have grafted you to Me? Let Me hear your voice again...."

How Splendid You are, Anointed One, Sacrificial Lamb of God, encircled by Your angels and all the saints. Irresistible One, Reflection of the Father, light thrice holy, One in Three, Three in One Light, Brighter than a thousand suns; how have I been deemed worthy of seeing the Son and in the Son the Father?

"Have you not heard My dove that the lowly will rejoice in Me and that the poorest will exult in My Presence? Have you not noticed My weakness I have for the wretched and how I delight to instruct the poor?"

My God, my God! who is this arising like dawn shimmering in the twilight, like the morning star? Who is this fairer than the moon, adorned with the sun and a Gate wide open in Her Heart?

"She is the Queen of Heaven, She is My Mother and your Mother, the loveliest of women, beautiful as Heaven, radiant as My Glory, unique in Her Perfection, the Delight of My Soul, She is the Woman with the twelve stars on Her Head for a crown, the Vessel of My Glory, a Reflection of My Eternal Light. She is the One whose Presence in My Courts outshines all the constellations put together. She is

291

the Vessel of the True Light, The Word, made flesh and who lived among you. She is Grace in Grace, and the Sweetest Song of the psalmists. She is My Theme of Joy, My Honour and My Boast. She is the Gate to Heaven, the One who shows Her children how to enter into My Kingdom. She is My Masterpiece. She is the Consoler of your Consoler, Co-Redemptress of your Redeemer, the Bride of My Holy Spirit. Daughter, I will take no rest; not until I take you, too, into My Mother's House; into the Room of Her who conceived me, to reveal to you, too, Her Beauty. Then, all the mysteries that seemed to you like a well of enigmas will suddenly, like a clap of lightning, be revealed to you, too, My beloved, and you will understand why the Woman clothed with the Sun descends now from My Courts to you all at a moment so obscure. Let your eyes, My dove, be fixed ahead; your gaze be straight before you. By the Path that I trod on I will return, My love. I will come and look after My Vineyard Myself. Emmanuel will be with you." (End)

...Do you like it?

Very!

Bless Me then; praise Me and love Me...

May Your Name be blessed and praised; May Love teach us to love Him; May we learn to seek You in simplicity of heart;

May Your Holy Spirit fill the whole world.

Let not one of Your flowers wither, but make them all bloom with a delicate fragrance to glorify You,

O Holy of Holies.

A message from "Our Lady, most Holy"

...I came from heaven in deep distress and in tears to let you know how distant you were from God; I came to you all to ask you to reconcile with God and with each other and to make no more distinctions between you,...

...I came to remind you all that a true apostle of God is the one who does the Will of God: to love is to do the Will of God;...

December 6 & 8, 1993

I 'i Panayia' (*'Our Lady, most Holy' in Greek*) am with you now, Daughter; Leave Jesus to model you into the image He desires you to be. By offering your will to My Son, Jesus Christ, and by offering yourself entirely, you truly please Him and His Will is being done in you. Do not be afraid; work with ardour and revive His Church. Let His creation realize that the Word is alive and untiringly active. I will, as your Mother, always encourage you to lift the Cross Jesus trusted you with. Now write, My daughter:

In these days more than any time, I have been giving messages to revive your faith and remind you of heavenly things. I have been continuously calling for Peace and spreading messages for Unity and Reconciliation between brothers. I came from heaven in deep distress and in tears to let you know how distant you were from God. I came to you all to ask you to reconcile with God and with each other and to make no more distinctions between you, "for everyone who calls on the Name of the Lord will be saved" (*Rm 10:12-13*). I have never failed anyone; I came in peace terms, even to the least of you, to proclaim God's Peace, and begged this generation to raise their eyes and search for God and offer sacrifices to God.

I came in your days where so many of you were estranged from the life of God. I came to remind you all that a true apostle of God is the one who does the Will of God:

To love is to do the Will of God

Vassula, I have been sent by God to cure many of you, but My calls have not been honoured nor highly placed. I was sent by the Most High to gather you in large crowds and teach you that love is the essence of all the Law. My daughter, My Soul is sad because the blessings from heaven are disregarded to this day. Failing to recognize the righteousness and the essence of the Message that comes from God, to this day men are trying to promote their own ideas. Thus the Word was skillfully withdrawn and My Footsteps concealed by human hand for fear of the lips of the world. If only they had put their hope in Me and trusted Me.... How much more would they have benefitted from the conversion of those whom they keep rejecting!

...Work, little one, for the Lord, allow Him to engrave on you His entire Plan. The days are coming when these questions will be raised by the Lord to every one of you:

"Have you loved your neighbour as yourself? Is it possible that you still have not understood God's Will? Have you done everything you can to maintain peace? When your enemy was hungry have you offered him to eat from your table? When he was thirsty, have you given him drink? How is it that what you give, you give it without love?" I have asked you for prayers; many of you pray, but without love. Many of you fast, but without love. So many of you speak of My messages, but very few follow them because love is missing in your hearts. **You bow low and follow the letter of the Law, but fail to understand the heart of the Law**. Many of you talk about unity, yet are first to condemn those who practice it because you have no love. If you practice all that I have been asking you without love, you are still in the dark; you are still for war and not for Peace. You believe you know everything, but in reality you know nothing. When I called out for reconciliation, since you are all parts of one another, I have not been heard. To this day I call out to all of you:

Live My messages!

Renew yourselves in God, in His Love and learn to love one another; be **good** and **holy**! Do not lie to yourselves, little children, following illusory desires. LOVE is to live in the Truth. Have you not read that "if you give away all that you possess, piece by piece, and if you even let them take your body to burn it, but are without love, it will do you no good whatever?" Have you not understood that if a single one of you is hurt, all parts of the Body of Christ are hurt and suffer with it? If you hurt your neighbour you hurt Christ's Body, not your neighbour. Can you say:

"I came to God with reverence, sincerity and love."

"When?" will He ask you, "when have you come to Me with reverence, sincerity and love? My Body, you have mutilated. I have been judged, treated with insult, calumny, and I have been betrayed by falsehood. I was despised and rejected, utterly disgraced by your lips, so, when have you come to Me with reverence, sincerity and love? I am asking you to give some definitive proof of your love for Me." My children, realize now why Satan has taken advantage of your weakness and tempted you to war. Christ has come to you hungry and you gave Him no food; He came to you thirsty and you gave Him no drink; He came to you as a stranger and you did not welcome Him but treated Him as you pleased. My children, your love is not to be merely words on your lips, but something that comes from your heart. Your love should be alive and active; I am with you to help you. I bless you all by saying: let everything you do be done with your heart, in love.

Prophesy on Russia

...I tell you, your sister Russia will be the head of many nations and will glorify Me in the end...

December 13, 1993

God, Lord Almighty, bind me more to you; bind me in Your Eternal Love.

I Am is with you and I shall never fail you; you are bound to Me.... Now I have called you and you responded; write, My Vassula:

Your sister Russia will honour Me in the very end and one day will be called holy for I shall be her Ruler. Once again, Integrity will live there....yes?

Lord, corruption is penetrating in her now....

I will lower her eyes....

I do not understand in which way, Lord, will You lower her eyes.

Very well, I will tell you then:

By the brilliance of My majesty[1] I will come and rest in her heart....

---

1. I understood by a purification, for when God reveals Himself and shines in a soul, the contrast of Light within darkness is so great that the soul sees vividly its imperfections and suffers a lot.

295

Lord, she still lives in the blackness of sin, and anguish.

Those who have taken the wrong turning will fall. I will destroy the luxurious forces with My Fire and the proud will be brought low. I intend to rebuild My House and I shall adopt her sons and daughters to honour Me. Vassula, do not just stand there bewildered and uncomprehending. I tell you, your sister Russia will be the head (spiritually) of many nations and will glorify Me in the end. Listen carefully and understand:

Her shepherds will be gathering

while treaties will be breaking elsewhere, and while rebellion will be working its way elsewhere to abolish the Perpetual Sacrifice; **Russia's shepherds will be gathering** to restore My House, reverencing the Perpetual Sacrifice, worshipping and honouring Me. When in the last days nation after nation will decline and pervert themselves for having erected the disastrous abomination in the Holy Place; **Russia's shepherds will be gathering** to sanctify her altars. And while others *(The apostates)* will be reverencing a lifeless form, an invention of human skill, an unbreathing image, **Russia's shepherds will be gathering,** glorifying Me. For I, God, will preserve her Integrity; and while efforts very evilly are being spent elsewhere to shorten the days of My mouthpieces, since they are the **hope** of this world, **Russia's shepherds will be gathering** to protect My Holy Sacrifice. I for My part, will be setting My Throne in her, and I will assemble all those who bear My Name together for My Glory.

I will repair her broken altars, for many who live under My Name will side up with her in the end, and her shepherds will, with one hand and one spirit, re-erect My tottering House. What had once been twisted will now be straightened, and I will adorn Russia with impressive vestments because of her zeal in Me. I will place her shepherds at the head of enumerable nations. I have engraved her with the seal of consecration to offer Me once more incense and an appeasing fragrance. This is why I will overwhelm her shepherds with miracles. "Russia, My Loyalty and My Gentleness will sanctify you; Russia, My daughter, **acknowledge Me entirely** and I promise you on oath to exalt your descendants like stars and give them sacred vestments. **Acknowledge Me entirely,** Russia, and I will annihilate all your opponents. I will, if you **acknowledge Me wholly,** do fresh wonders in you to prove to everyone living under the sun, My Mercy and My Holiness." I am ready to show My Compassion on her and I will not be slow if she welcomes Me eagerly. I will not delay to show her how I, the Almighty, can eliminate the arrogant and break their lawless sceptres.

But,[1] if she will perverse the liberty I have just given her and will put Me out of her mind, even for just a while, I will allow an enemy to invade her.... If Russia will not come back to Me with **all her heart** and **acknowledge Me** with an undivided heart, as her Saviour, I will send a vast and mighty host in her and from her to all nations. A host such as has never been before; such as will never be again to the remotest ages. The sky will turn black and will tremble, and the stars will lose their brilliance.... "Today I am ready to make up to you, Russia, for the years you suffered, and I can still snatch you all from the blaze, **were you to acknowledge Me fully.** Seek good and not evil. Have you already forgotten your famine and your drought? *(Spiritually)*....

I have pushed back the red dragon and destroyed the luxuriance of his empire. I humbled the proud. I have opened the prison gates and freed your captives. I overthrew the kingdom of the red dragon that had coiled in your womb, that one that made the earth tremble turning your land into a wasteland. To honour My Name again in you, I have opened your Churches one after the other. I called you by your name that Day:

Russia, *(From USSR to Russia)*

to rejoice and be glad, and to celebrate the Feast of My Transfiguration.[2] I transfigured your image instantly. Your misery of oppression was your punishment for the crimes of the world; and now I am waiting to be gracious to you, Russia, for in the end you will glorify Me.

I tell you, while others will be destroying, you will be building.

---

1. Suddenly God's Voice dropped and became sad and very grave. It saddened me profoundly.
2. The Lord predicted to transfigure Russia in Message. The fall of the communism happened in the week of the Orthodox Feast of Transfiguration.

While many will be falling, your shepherds will be rising, **if** you put your trust in Me. And, while some of My Own, sitting at table with Me, will be wickedly betraying Me, **you** will be the one who will stretch out your hand to defend My Name, My Honour and My Sacrifice. So every one of your sins will have been paid. You will then step forward, loyally, and save your brother; your brother who was the prey of the evil one. You will resurrect the Church into One, and Justice will come to live in Her. Justice will bring Peace and everlasting security. Happy will you be, singing praises to Me. Rich will you be, for the loyalty you showed towards your King. He will repay you a hundredfold; and there where treaties were broken, prophets despised and killed, there where much offense was sown and threats pronounced reaching the heavens with an uproar, there, My beloved, there your shepherds' nobel voices will call out: "**Salvation!** Priests and ministers of the Most High; salvation will only be found in Love! **Peace!** Shepherds of the Reflection of the Father; peace will only be found in Forgiveness. **Unity!** Unity, brothers of the Light thrice holy and Who is One in Three, Three in One Light, will only be found by intermarrying! May our Lord Almighty, the Irresistible One, render us worthy of His Name, may He grant us to be one in His Name. Eternal Father, let us be so completely one that the rest of the world will realize that it was You who sent the Sacrificial Lamb to glorify You and have Your Name known." Thus you will ravage the Divider and you will repair what had been undone. Russia, your role is to honour Me and glorify Me. The Festivity has yet to come, but it depends on you in which manner that Day will come:

do not let Me make you return to Me by fire, but with bonds of Peace.

Book of Daniel

...the book of Daniel that was sealed and the words in it kept secret are now being revealed to you all in their fullness;...

December 20, 1993

My Lord?

I Am;

Let the eyes of those who do not see Your signs remain no longer closed. Let the ears that no longer hear, open and become alert.

Let the heart that never understands Your Wisdom open and understand Your proverbs...Let their spirit cultivate all that You Yourself planted to glorify You.

I shall visit you all in the end...[1] and you, My daughter, do not let discouragement take the best of you; your race is not yet finished, so do not diminish your speed. I will help you and My Voice you shall hear to hearten your soul. Listen now and write: in the beginning when you did not know what Integrity meant, in the beginning before Wisdom came to instruct you My Word, I had sent you in those days My servant Daniel (*My guardian angel*) to touch your heart and bring you to Me. I thus came to raise one of the lowest of mankind.

It was by My Grace and Strength I made you Mine. Sovereignty dined with you and used you as His harp to enchant many of His household with His Love Hymn. Rejoice daughter, for I mean to complete your life's journey with you!

In the beginning, before My Fire crossed through you, I had sent My servant Daniel to ask you to read the book of Daniel for in it are relevant truths; truths and prophecies that should be unsealed to be understood, then proclaimed. They are the signs of the end of times, therefore, the book of Daniel that was sealed and the words in it kept secret are now being revealed to you all in their fullness. I have been saying to all of you that your generation has apostatized and that this apostasy would creep into the heart of My Sanctuary affecting priests, bishops and cardinals. You see, daughter, I am talking about those apostates who are betraying My Church and are opposing My chosen one, the Vicar of My Church who holds their rebellion back. But it was said that Satan will set to work in your times to destroy all that is good and will spring in pursuit of those whom I am sending you with My Merciful calls, that could have saved you. My calls and

---

1. I understood: By fire. God will visit us all by fire and everyone will listen, see and understand.

299

My signs from Heaven have not been grasped by those apostates but are rejected; yet everything evil that can lead their soul into further darkness and destruction will be welcomed by them instead. They would welcome the Lie and reject the Truth. It has been said *(Dn 7:25)* that, for a time, two times and a half time *(Meaning: Three and a half years.)*, My people would be under their persecution and the dominion of the beast *(Ap 13:1-18)*. It has been said that they will, with the help of this beast, consider changing the Traditions and My Law and are planning to remove the Perpetual Sacrifice, trample it underfoot and crush it and in its place erect the disastrous abomination, a lifeless image.... And every saint I am sending you in your generation will be put into their power.

Today you are all watching how these prophecies are being fulfilled. Influenced by the beast, these apostates[1] are making war on every saint I am sending you, proving today to be the stronger *(Dn 7:21)*, than those[2] who reject My calls of today with no reason at all. In My Day they will make this confession:

(Read Dn 9:4-19) "O Lord, we have been blind and we have sinned. We have indeed wronged You and we have betrayed Your commandments and Your Law. We have refused to listen to Your servants the prophets who spoke in Your Name to all the world. Lord, we have not listened to Your Merciful Calls nor taken any counsel. God, we paid no attention to Your manifest signs. We have been ridiculing all of them because we have sinned against You. We flouted Scriptures. Had we not, we would have accepted Your Sign in Heaven[3] and the gifts of Your Holy Spirit. But we turned our eyes away not to see lest we see and get converted. And the curse and imprecation written in Scriptures will come pouring down on us now—because we have indeed sinned against You; and now, now that the Holy Sacrifice has been abolished, to whom can we turn? On

---

1. The apostates are those, according to Our Lord, ecclesiastics influenced by the Freemasons. These apostates are noted in Ap. 13:11. They are as the 2nd beast, alias the false prophet.
2. The good shepherds, but skeptical and closed.
3. Mt 24:30 Dn 7:13-14 I understood the following: Manifestation from the Holy Spirit that comes now with power, gathering God's people. The outpouring of the Holy Spirit is a Heavenly Sign to renew the Church; in other words to establish the New Jerusalem.

what can we feed our souls? How could we quench our thirst? How could we obtain Life now? All the desolation of the abomination You predicted, but kept secret, has now come true. Our distress is unparalleled, since we first came into existence *(Dn 12:1).*"[1]

Vassula, My Love will sustain you. Allow Me, My dearest soul, ever so fragile, to use you entirely. Be My silent witness *(By writing).* Come.

The Sign of the Son of Man appearing now in Heaven

...ah, generation, how could you ask for more signs, more than the Sign of the Son of Man that I am giving you today?...

December 23, 1993

Master, the fig tree will begin to form its figs, and the vines will start blossoming.

No, My bride, the fig tree has already formed its figs and the vines have already blossomed. Daughter, can you not see? Have you not noticed My Sign in heaven *(Allusion to Mt 24:30)*? Hear and write:

Generation, I have been sending you and I am still sending you My angels[2] to gather My chosen from the four winds, from one end of heaven to the other, to stand ready because the Bridegroom soon will step out from heaven and will be with you. Your world of today will wear out quickly. I am sending you, My angels, to gather My elect, My people, to renew My Church. Have you not noticed? Have you not understood? Do you still not perceive My Sign?

Today My Holy Spirit raptures one out of two, enwraps him in His blazing Fire and sends him out to be a witness to the Most High.

---

1. The Lord stopped His dictation but had not finished His message due to its length. I understood that He will continue later.

2. Angels here stands for: messengers. The chosen ones sent by God to the world, carrying His Word.

My Holy Spirit lifts one while leaving another one behind in the dust among dust. One is taken, one left. My Holy Spirit, like the wind, blows wherever it pleases. You hear its sound but you cannot tell where it comes from or where it is going. My Holy Spirit, like a Bridegroom, appears in your days, to court you, seduce you and wed you. My Holy Spirit is laid like a precious cornerstone in your heart, to be the foundation stone of your faith, of your hope, of your love and of your zeal for Me, your God.

My Holy Spirit, in your days, blows on you this way and that way. His Breath is like a stream flowing in every direction, and everywhere this stream flows, fruit trees sprout up with leaves that never wither but are medicinal, and everyone who eats from them is healed. Yes, My Holy Spirit is a life-giving spring, the inner Power of My Kingdom, raising disciples of Wisdom. My Holy Spirit builds, renews and embellishes; but the Deceiver destroys and batters to death all that is holy. How is it that you cannot perceive the dazzling Light of My Holy Spirit? Like the Light of seven days in one, My Holy Spirit shines today in heaven. Is this Sign of the Son of Man appearing in heaven *(Mt 24:30)* not enough for you?

Like a shepherd gathering his flock, My Holy Spirit gathers and saves the dispersed flock. I am revealing things hidden and unknown to you, generation, at the favorable time I am revealing you these things. Whether you turn right or left you will see the dazzling Sign in heaven of My Holy Spirit and your ears will hear: "I Am He!" *(Jn 18:6 and 8)* I Am is with you in heart. I Am is here to build your hopes, your strength, your faith and your love. My child, "koumi!" rise now you who have perished long ago; rise now, My child, and take your place. Here is a shepherd's staff; I will direct your soul to receive instruction: go out now and look for the rest of My strayed sheep. Weary not on the way, My child, and if you do I shall carry you on My Shoulders. Today, I Myself will rally My sheep....

Ah, generation, how could you ask for more signs, more than the Sign of the Son of Man that I am giving you today? What man cannot, indeed, see My intentions? I speak the Truth, yet you do not believe that it is I who speaks. How is it you cannot grasp My Voice? Have you ever asked yourselves how have the paths of those living in the dust been straightened? Have you asked yourselves who was it who opened the mouths of the dumb and gave Wisdom's speech to the ignorant? And who was it who instructed the poor in spirit, the wretched as you call them? Have you not heard that My Holy Spirit is indeed the Life-Giver? Have you not understood how My Holy Spirit shuns in the presence of the proud of heart, but reveals His intimacy to the lowly?

My Holy Spirit today is given to you as a Great Sign in heaven (*Allusion to Mt 24:30*), a reflection of My Return. So long as your thoughts remain earthly you will be unable to grasp the things that are in heaven. Have you not read: "Yahweh will appear above them and His arrow will flash like lightning" (*Zc 9:14*). "See how Yahweh comes in fire? To assuage His anger with burning, His threats with flaming fire; (*Is 66:15*) the works of My Father are being carried out. Listen and understand: I have said that I will be coming to gather the nations of every language. Many of you ask: "when is this going to happen and what will be the sign of Your coming?"

I had forewarned you that when you would see the disastrous abomination, of which the prophet Daniel spoke, set up in the Holy Place, that is, when you see the Enemy[1] take his place where he ought not to be, and that is: in My Sanctuary, My Dwelling Place (*Dwelling place: soul*). When you see this Rebel (*The Antichrist—as set forth above*) claiming to be so much greater than all that men call 'god', so much greater than anything that is worshipped, **that he enthrones himself in My Sanctuary**[2] and claims that he is God,[3] Yes Vassula! Know that this was a foresign given before the Sign of the Son of Man appearing now in heaven to save you.

Lift your heads and look at the sky for My heavenly Manna. Stand erect, hold your heads high, because your liberation is at hand. How is it that My Holy Spirit cannot be noticed among so many of you?

---

1. The Antichrist; today there are many antichrists, for they have as their guide, the spirit of Rebellion, which installed itself in the innermost part of their soul, there, where God ought to dwell.

2. Allusion to Dn 11:31 and 8:11 and 12:11 and Mt 24:15.

3. As I said before, Jesus says to us that today already these signs are here: many antichrists, nevertheless, this prophecy of the Perpetual Sacrifice abolished, will come concretely: when the Apostasy and rebellion will be generalized, then **the Antichrist**, who is already among us will appear openly.

The deep and the earth tremble at My visitation so do not say anymore that justice is not being done, and that the Ark of the covenant[1] is far away. The Ark of the Covenant is right above you in the sky so that you witness My Glory.

If you eat from My Manna you will revive—you will be born again. So do not look for other signs. Have you not heard that it is the Spirit that gives life? If certain among you do not believe, it is because you have not eaten this Manna. Yes, it is My Holy Spirit who could give you an untarnished understanding to My mysteries. This heavenly food is the food of the poor and it is not bought with money.[2] Sanctify yourselves and purify yourselves to enter the Garden, which is My Kingdom. I am giving you today this Sign of My Holy Spirit in heaven. It fills the whole world, and makes all things new; deploying His strength from one end of the earth to the other, and yet, many of you defy My Mercy and venture to say:

"Where are the signs from God? There is no Sign of the Son of Man appearing in heaven to prove to us that Sovereignty is at our gates." You lie in wait for My Spirit-anointed-ones since they annoy you and oppose your way of thinking! Yes, the very sight of them weigh your spirit down. Ah...and the root of your understanding is decaying....I tell you: My Holy-Spirit-anointed-ones may appear to you frail, but they are well rooted in Me; hardly grown, but they are grafted on Me; and like an untarnished mirror I move them about, to flash My words everywhere and wherever they may be. I Am; and they will continue to flash My Words to you all, to lead you into My Kingdom. They will continue to reveal My Power even though you deal with them harshly. They will bear insult and calumny humbly to save you. They will not open their mouth to contradict you in the sight of all the nations, but, will be like angels whose feet bring good news. They will continue to flash My Word like an untarnished

---

1. Heb 9:4 The Ark of the Covenant contained a jar. Inside the jar was kept the manna that fell from heaven to feed Moses and the Jews while crossing the desert.—Jesus makes an allusion to this manna to talk about His Holy Spirit: as Celestial Manna.

2. The rich in spirit cannot receive the Kingdom of God. Allusion to the beatitude: Blessed are the poor in spirit, theirs is the Kingdom of heaven.

mirror proclaiming Salvation and heralding Peace and Love. And though they will be despised and rejected by many, they will bear their sufferings with dignity. Lift up your eyes to the heavens and discern My Sign. I am coming to restore My House. I am coming to renew you, generation. I am revealing My Holy Face to you all, to save you. O Come! you who still waver. I tell you; from the beginning I have never spoken to you obscurely, and all the time these things have been happening.

I have been always present—

and you, daughter, keep yourself untarnished so that My Light may reach to the ends of the earth. Preach with accuracy all that My Spirit is giving you. I will encourage you, My daughter and My Own. Your Spouse is with you.

Icon of Saint Michael

from Saint Michael's Monastery on the Island of Simi in Greece

Messages from St. Michael and Daniel

March 5, 1987

I read St. Michael's prayer to him.

Prayer to St. Michael

St. Michael, the archangel, defend us in the day of battle; be our safeguard against the wickedness and snares of the devil.

May God rebuke him, we humbly pray, and do thou, O prince of the heavenly host, by the power of God, cast into hell, Satan, and all the other evil spirits, who prowl through the world seeking the ruin of souls. Amen.

St. Michael answered me:

With God's power I, St. Michael, will cast into hell Satan and all other evil spirits that ruin the souls.

May 17, 1987

I read St. Michael's prayer:

Read the next one.

I read The Memorare of St. Bernard. (St Mary)

Remember, O most gracious Virgin Mary, that never was it known that anyone who fled to your protection, implored your help, or sought your intercession, was left unaided.

Inspired with this confidence, I fly unto you. O Virgin of Virgins, my Mother! To you I come, before you I stand sinful and sorrowful. O Mother of the Word Incarnate, despise not my petitions, but in your mercy, hear and answer me. Amen.

February 26, 1988

Glory be to God, Praise the Lord

(These words were uttered by St. Michael when I prayed to him....)

April 27-29, 1988

Praised be the Lord! Glory be to God

St. Michael said 'praised be the Lord' after reading his prayer and St. Mary said 'Glory be to God' after reading her prayer

September 29, 1988

Raphael? Gabriel & Michael

Glory be to the Most High, (*I prayed to St. Michael*) for He has raised you up from the dead; you are to be on your guard always from Satan, recollect yourself before the Lord; pray to me, *the Prayer of St. Michael, exorcism?* Yes, if God's creation only knew how this prayer combats evil, they would have recited it daily; be prepared for the Lord's word always, the Eternal One loves you, praise Him! *Ah, St. Michael, Thank You for guarding & combatting for us.*

February 27, 1989

Peace be with you, *(St. Michael)*

March 1, 1989

St. Michael's Message for the reunion (meeting)

Vassula, Glory be to God! Praised be the Lord! The Lord's Mercy is Boundless, the Lord's Grace is upon you. Awake! Awake! Come back to the Lord all those who have abandoned the Truth, return and repent! Pray for the conversion of your brethern, take heed upon the Lord's warnings. Peace, peace, make peace with God! I, Saint Michael, am near you, to defend you. Pray without cease; your prayers are needed more than ever these days of Lent; I bless you in the Name of the Father and of the Son and of the Holy Spirit, amen.

March 6, 1989

Peace, I am your angel Daniel, I am with you guiding you, I am doing the Lord's Will, I am praying for you without cease. Desire the Lord, accept all that He gives you, beware of evil.

chase away evil when it's near me please!

I do. Pray My Vassula with fervour for this is the way the Lord likes it, never cease praying, come, be in Peace.

March 8, 1989

I love you all to folly, remember always this; I will relent My Justice only when tremendous reparations will be done.

ΙΧΘΥΣ ⸙

Love loves you: here is Saint Michael, child of God, nothing is impossible to God; tremendous reparations are to be done; if your generation converts, the Holy of Holies will relent His Punishment. Let those who have ears hear, for His Mercy reaches from age to age for those who fear Him; be alert, never cease repairing; those that mock you now will grind their teeth later on; I, Saint Michael, pray without cease for this evil generation. Pray child, and obey the Lord; praise the Lord for the outpouring of His Spirit among you all.

St. Michael, thank you,

Peace to you.

April 5, 1989

Here is Saint Michael: children of God, do not listen nor conversate with Satan, to lie is to conversate with the demon, to accumulate anger in you, is to give the devil a foothold, do not let your tongue be the cause of your falls; pray to Me and I shall intercede for you; have confidence in God and in His Infinite Mercy; I bless you all.

July 4, 1989

(Saint Michael is giving us a message.)

I am Saint Michael; I am your Saint Michael, to whom you pray for protection and for defending you against the evil one, have no fear, your hardships will be redressed by this prayer. Allow the Spirit of Love to expand His Calls of Grace, listen to the Spirit of Grace, listen to the Spirit for His Mercy is Great; do not suffocate those who receive the Holy One's Messages like your ancestors, by saying to the seers: "see no visions" and to the prophets, "do not prophecy to us for **we** are in the Truth." Instead, lift up your eyes and look around, all are assembling and coming back to God, your sons from far away and your daughters being tenderly carried, for the Lord has announced this: though night dominates your era, My Light shall pierce it and will cover this earth and all nations shall come to Me and My flock. I will gather again into one Holy Fold under My Holy Name; pray O children of the Lord and allow the Lord to redress His People by accepting what comes out of the babe's mouth and the lowly. Have no fear, Salvation is near and at your very gates. I bless you in the Name of the Father and of the Son and of the Holy Spirit, amen.

Allow the Lord to use you, Vassula, yearn for the Lord. Love Him for He is most Compassionate.

November 14, 1989

"Alleluia our Anointed One! *(This came from angels' voices).* Delight the Lord and seek Him in purity of heart, seek Him in simplicity of heart, we are your angels who guard you without cease;" God loves you and I, Daniel, *(Daniel my guardian angel)* am always with you. Stay small for this is what pleases the Lord!

Ah Daniel...how can I avoid the meetings where people start to know the revelation and me, how can I stay 'small?' You know how I dislike being exposed!

Vassula, stay small means remain humble and pleasing to the Lord. Remember it is the Lord's wish you assemble, *(the monthly prayer meetings).* Have no fear, His message should be known. The world ought to come and meet the **King of Peace**. Your generation should recognize God and be converted. Give thanks to God for His Merciful Works. I, Daniel, pray without cease for you. God wants you to be good. Reveal His Love to all mankind without fear. The Most High blesses you and all those who commit themselves in this Message to announce It to the nations. Love loves you all.

ΙΧΘΥΣ ➤⊙

January 9, 1991

(I wept for all the false accusations said about me by "_____" and that damage so much.)

Flower, this is My Cross too, but allow Me to treat you as I please. Your love reaches Me as incense. When a sudden deadly scourge descends on you, My child, offer it to Me; I shall make good use of it. Nations are at the verge of war, do you understand? Little one, offer Me your sufferings, because there is an anger ready to flame...have My Peace...have confidence in Me, My Vassula, remember, I shall comfort you. Then there is your angel by your side to console you and dress your wounds; but for the time being allow Me to leave My Cross on you. Courage, daughter! My Cross is heavy and weighing on you, but I know that you will be willing to carry It till the end. I the Lord bless you. I shall reward you in heaven. *(Daniel, my angel)* Your Jesus loves you. It is I, Daniel. Remember, the Lord has rested you, but now, would you not want to rest Him too? Vassula, satisfy Him then, and allow Him to crush you with sufferings. There is a big price to pay for Peace, there are many lives at stake; how often does the Lord crush you with such a weight? *Not often.* No, not many times; so the few times He does, accept them and do not be vehement about it. Vassula, all these sacrifices are not going in vain; they fortify you as well. Remain in God's Love.

> Eager He is, to purify you,
> eager be, to glorify Him.

—Daniel, your angel

(I smiled. Somehow my angel always manages to make me smile. I smiled at the prose he has written. That is typical of my angel.)

311

September 29, 1991 *(St. Michaels Feast)*

St. Michael:

I love you child of God; trust Me.

The Lord: Rest in My Heart, I the Lord bless you. Come, My Heart is your nest.

August 27, 1992 *(Simi-Panormiti)*

Vassula, listen to My Archangel whom you came to visit: Child of God, do not fear, stand firm when they persecute you. You are not alone. Give your True Shepherd all your problems and He will guide and lead you and the Mighty One has His Hand on you. Listen when He speaks for He has great plans on you. He is the living God and there is no one above Him. I shall help everyone who is willing to overcome the Evil One and in the Father through the Father I will undo the work of the devil. Let anyone who wants to boast, boast of the Lord! Praised be the Lord; remain in His Heart and remember, He has truly spoken to you. God's Archangel Michael.

September 29, 1993 *(Feast of the Archangels)*

Saint Michael gave me this message:

God is King of the whole earth and heaven; there is no one like Him! He is your salvation, your strength and your peace. In your distress He will stretch out His Hand to lift you and save you. God is Master of the Heavens and the earth, and there is no one like Him, no one you can compare Him with. I tell you: stay awake because no one knows the day when your Master is coming to you. The Almighty One will not prolong His decision. He shall come to you all in a Pillar of Fire and the light of His people will become a fire and your Holy One a Flame burning and devouring the shrewdness of evil *(Allusion to the Purification)*. His Light will penetrate and pierce Darkness and those who could not see will see. He will destroy the proud of the present world. The remnant left will be His Own. It will be so scarce that even a child would be able to count it **unless the Almighty One hears from the earth a cry of repentance!** His sentence is just. Remain in the Lord, Vassula; and He will give you strength. I will guard you.

October 14, 1994

Message from St. Michael

Vassula-of-Christ's-Passion, I, Saint Michael the Archangel, greet you and bless you. Remember how God called you to live a True Life in Him? The memory only of your spiritual resurrection to this day touches Me to tears... You were once at war with God since all your concern was on what is unspiritual. But, now, glory be to God, the Just, the Most High, has covered you with His Holy Spirit and with His powerful hand lifted you to become a witness of His Holy Spirit. Since His Spirit made His Home in you, and from the beginning (*the beginning of my conversion*), His Spirit finding His Home in you, glorifies Himself by listening to your cry of: Father, "Abba."

It will not be long now when He will descend to pull down iniquity that installed itself in man's heart. Look here, for over three years the perpetual sacrifice (*The real Presence of Jesus in the Eucharist.*) will be trampled. For this reason of incredible blasphemy, a third of your inhabitants shall die of iniquity. The Lord swore this by His Holiness.

Prepare yourself to meet God now. (*He was asking me to meet God in this way.*)

(*When he saw my sadness, St. Michael decided to stay a bit more with me.*)

I have told you all this with no pleasure, for the Devil today, in your generation, is given great honours. He was a murderer from the beginning and a liar, and now he is worshipped as a father. The honours are given to him instead. In your days, they bow down before his works and in this way, your generation, has drawn down punishment on themselves. Your countries are infested by legions of unclean spirits that roam everywhere. Satan today is tempting even the elect of God. This is why trouble is coming to this generation who constructs its towers with innocent blood (*Abortion law legalized in many nations.*) and founds its homelands on crime. This sacrifice (*The abortion pleases Satan, because Satan needs human sacrifice to gain*

313

power, and this is done daily with many not even being aware that it becomes a cult to the Devil.) alone pleases Satan....

Put your trust in the Most High, child, and encourage people to ask for My Intercession. I, Saint Michael, the Archangel of God will never weary of defending the truth. Stand your ground, (*St. Michael was trying to tell me to "copy" him, that means, never to get weary or feel discouraged in spite of the blows I receive.*) even though the enemy's blows on you can be traumatic, I am with you.

Enjoy the favour of the Most High.

In Prayer
St. Michael, the Archangel

Sculptured in Sussex Oak
by Claire Sheridan
Photo: Courtesy of Black Rock College, Dublin, Ireland